No
Bullshit
Strategy

No
Bullshit
Strategy

A Founder's Guide to Gaining Competitive
Advantage with a Strategy that Actually Works

Alex M H Smith

Matador
Unit E2 Airfield Business Park,
Harrison Road, Market Harborough,
Leicestershire. LE16 7UL
Tel: 0116 279 2299
Email: books@troubador.co.uk
Web: www.troubador.co.uk/matador
Twitter: @matadorbooks

ISBN 978 1803136 516

British Library Cataloguing in Publication Data.
A catalogue record for this book is available from the British Library.

Typeset in 10pt EBGaramond by Troubador Publishing Ltd, Leicester, UK

Matador is an imprint of Troubador Publishing Ltd

For C&C

Author's note

I didn't want to bore you (or myself) with pages and pages of detailed case studies about businesses you've never heard of just to make a simple point. Therefore I've tried to illustrate the principles in this book with quick references to big brands we're all familiar with. Are my explanations historically accurate? I've no idea, I wasn't there, but probably not. However, I'm not a historian or academic so who cares – the point is never the example; the point is the *principle* the example is illustrating. So long as you get what I'm talking about, it's done its job.

As you'll discover, that's what strategy is all about: seeing the big-picture truth that transcends mundane factual detail. So with that in mind, let's get on with it.

Contents

Foreword

by Tom Goodwin

We love the idea that the world is more complex than ever. That AI or 5G or Big Data will change everything. That "things are different now". We generate new terms, jump on every new idea, and try hard to escape the vulnerability of the mundane by adding nonsense in all directions.

This makes it hard to see the wood for the trees. And harder still to be bold and decisive.

We see this everywhere, manifested as fear. It seems more and more people in corporations are seeking to hide. Deferring to others, avoiding decision making, and seeking data less to illuminate than to provide insurance against blame.

We need to change this cultural fixation on safety and not being noticed, and instead start getting noticed for brilliance, imagination, and ambition.

This is what this book is for. A way for leaders to have the confidence it takes to seek such brilliance. It's a guide, a compass, a torchlight, a map, (and if you've got the physical book, perhaps an excellent firelighter, not that you'd want to burn it), which cuts through the noise and illuminates the path to effective strategy, and the kind of decisiveness that remains our key to progress.

Within these pages, you will find a bold and necessary departure from the complex and abstract theories that often dominate modern business literature. Instead, you're taken by the hand and led through a clear, relevant and inspiring journey of clear thinking and brave execution.

For almost all of human civilization we've lived in an age of scarcity. But in the modern age we're more likely to die of obesity than starvation, more likely to drown than die of thirst, more likely to get too much information than feel under informed - and above all else suffer from too much choice. Living in the modern age then is to be overwhelmed, and that's what this book stands against – a switch to more focused leadership, based not simply on what we "could" make, but on what consumers truly need.

This might be the most interesting time there has ever been to drive corporate growth, and when we step back we can see it's the best time there has ever been to work in. So with that sense of optimism and excitement, go forth, and create your path to prosper.

Introduction

The issue of bullshit in strategy

Most strategy is, let's face it, bullshit. And I mean that in the most technical sense.

Bullshit can be best described as a bunch of fancy words that ultimately mean nothing. And for the most part, strategy can be described that way too. We all know it – even if perhaps we don't want to be the one to stick our head above the parapet and say it.

First, few of us actually really know what "strategy" is. It's a corporate buzzword which is suitably vague as to mean whatever we want it to mean, and hence nothing at all. Like the very best varieties of bullshit, it can be inserted pretty much at random into any declaration to give it an air of weight and authority, without us needing to worry that we'll be called out on it. This confusion is something I experience on a near daily basis: when I tell someone I'm a "strategist" they look at me as if I'd told them I'm a pixie – invariably following up with something like, "Errr, OK, what do you mean by that exactly?"

Second, even if someone does more or less understand and respect "strategy" in the *abstract*, that doesn't mean that they have much time for actual *strategies* themselves. Sure, we can all agree that "strategy" is this big important thing, but how many of us have come across an actual real-life strategy which we truly found helpful?

Generally the best-case scenario for a strategy we might encounter, is that it's merely a harmless bundle of verbiage, that doesn't get too much in the way of the "proper" running of the business.

Considering all this, it's little wonder that – by my conservative estimate – about 98% of businesses are getting by with *no strategy at all* (though this might be news to some of them).

Heck, many of them are even extremely successful. Strategy is by no means a prerequisite to results, let me assure you.

And yet.

Despite the general uselessness of strategy, anyone who's picked up this book will know that underneath all the guff, there is something to it. That whilst it may not be a prerequisite for success, it does still tend to be present in the most extraordinary of achievements. That it brings your company's fate into your own hands, rather than leaving it to the mercies of chance. That it gives you a platform for long-term growth. That it creates businesses that are smooth-running and effortlessly profitable. That, in short, it is the factor that separates the legendary companies – the ones we always talk about – from the legions of merely adequate ones.

Strategy – in its rare, non-bullshitty forms – is the secret sauce that elevates business to an art, and that has the power to create extraordinary brands who stand out like beacons in their categories and have no competition.

If that's what you're into then this book is for you. It'll wash away all the crap and confusion, leaving you only with *pure strategic sauce*, presented in a manner that you can internalise and action right away.

To do this, there are two "flavours" of bullshit we're going to address:

1. No "bullshit strategy"

First and most obviously, we're going to address the issue of "bullshit strategy" – i.e. strategies that are just generally bad in some way.

Speaking broadly, these fall into three camps, which represent the vast majority of what's produced under the strategy banner on any given day:

BS Strategy 1: Goals as strategy
I'd like to think that most people who are reading this book would not fall for this one, as it's the most egregious strategic sin.

Simply put, many strategies aren't just bad; *they're not strategies at all*. Rather they are typically goals instead, e.g.:

"Our strategy is to become the number-one printer paper brand in the UK."

"Our strategy is to double our turnover."

"Our strategy is to revolutionise the toenail clipper industry."

Etc.

OK, that's fine, *but how exactly are you going to do that*? As you can see, such "strategies" generate more questions than answers – which is pretty much the exact opposite of what a strategy should actually do.

Surprisingly – despite so many people taking the piss out of it – this error is still extremely common. And in fairness it's easier to slip into than you might think. So we'll nip that one right in the bud.

BS Strategy 2: Generic strategies

A slightly more sophisticated form of bad strategy is that of the generic – in other words strategies which may be *functional*, but which are shared by pretty much all the other brands in your category.

As we shall see, the whole point of a strategy is that it sends you on a *different path from anyone else*. If you're not going to do that, then why bother strategising at all? Just cut out the middleman and straight up copy your competitors. Easy.

Unfortunately founders tend to be really good at rationalising that what they're doing is, in fact, "unique", and that their competitors aren't doing it at all. They'll say things like:

"The problem with all the other chocolate on the market is that it tastes terrible. That's why our strategy is to make chocolate that tastes really good!"

You think I'm exaggerating, but I've heard many strategies that pretty much boil down to that kind of logic. Trust me, when you're through with this, you'll be able to sniff out that bullshit before it even comes up.

BS Strategy 3: Fluffy meaningless confusing waffly unactionable strategies

Perhaps the most common strain of bullshit (in part because it contains the other two types of BS strategy), can be found in strategies that you simply can't do anything with because they're basically nonsense.

Generally we're talking here of your run-of-the-mill corporate guff, you know the kind of thing, "leverage synergies", "inspire the incredible", "deliver the extraordinary", and what have you.

Essentially this is anything that leaves you thinking, "OK, but what does that mean?" or, "OK, so what do I do with that?"

You've got to keep in mind that the only job a strategy really has, when you get right down to it, is to provoke specific action. Otherwise it's just words on a PowerPoint deck, and it needn't exist at all. I would even go so far as to say that a strategy's effectiveness in provoking action is more important than it being "right". After all, a "wrong-but-actionable" strategy will still produce positive moves in the market, which might succeed in unpredictable ways, whereas a "right-but-unactionable" strategy will produce nothing.

As you shall see, we will put as much emphasis here on the *delivery* and *shaping* of a strategy as we will on the intellectual content, meaning that you'll always be able to come up with something which people fundamentally "get". A necessity, I'm sure you'll agree.

2. "No bullshit" strategy

The second way this book will de-bullshitify strategy for you is not to do with the technicalities of the strategy itself, but rather in the way that it teaches it.

As I'm sure you know there are no shortage of strategy books out there, and for the most part their intellectual content is truly excellent. However, they tend to also be dry, dense, academic, technical, and just flat out *boring* – so the substance of their message never quite gets through.

They also tend to assume their reader is the CEO of Halliburton, or runs a pig iron mine in Peru, or perhaps has a unicorn tech startup on their hands and it's still 2012. It's all very *Harvard Business Review* kind of stuff – which is fine if that's what you're into, but that's not my game here.

I instead wanted to write for founders who are just like my clients: young, non-corporate, and don't fancy reading a book from an MBA syllabus in their free time.

We're going to arrive in a similar place to those classic strategy texts, sure, but via a completely different path – much more direct, intuitive, and principles-based. Our focus here is not to help you ace a test or dazzle the board with jargon, but rather generate killer insights that will transform the path of your business instantly.

There are no fancy models or flowcharts or proprietary systems or anything rigid you have to slot into here. Instead we're mostly going to be talking about fresh ways of seeing your business and its market which will unlock massive value for you.

To give you an example of what I mean, think about the old strategic insight that drove Starbucks' success, which they called "The Third Space". This was their term for "the space between work and home", where you're in a more comfortable and relaxed environment than the office but are still being creative and productive. This is what they wanted to create with their cafes, and what influenced them to introduce industry-defining innovations such as providing power outlets for laptops, and letting people stay for hours even if they only ordered one cup of coffee.

We take all that stuff for granted now, but back in the day it was pretty radical.

Can you see how that simple insight, the identification of a need for such a kind of space, shaped everything that Starbucks did, and drove their stellar growth? And can you also see how clear, direct, and compelling it is? How you could describe it to anyone in the pub and they'd totally get it – let alone people in the Starbucks team?

***That's* a strategy.**

That's something that will shape the entire direction of a business. That makes everything fall into place. That creates real value. And that changes the way people think about an industry. It's rough, big-picture, and totally transformative.

And it's the kind of thing we're going to generate right here.

A couple of notes about the layout of this book before we begin

Before getting cracking, there are two things I want you to bear in mind.

1. This isn't a book about "one big idea"; it's about lots of little ones

Many books in the strategy field have a central "theory" which they try to codify into a process or framework, and then sell to you. For instance a classic one is "finding your why".

This book isn't like that.

You see the problem with such "big idea" forms of strategy is that they tend to work brilliantly 20% of the time, and not at all 80% of the time. This is because not all effective strategies can be "boxed" into one model or structure. Using the "why" example, for instance, I've worked with brands where our strategy naturally fell into a why-like framework – but then equally I've worked with brands that had no why at all. The structure just didn't quite "fit".

(To be fair a why isn't meant to be a strategy at all, as we'll come on to, but I'm just illustrating a point for now.)

Lots of brands don't get this, and waste loads of energy trying to conform their strategy to whatever book the CEO happened to be reading that week. But this is often futile. There is simply no one way of doing things.

Consequently I'm not going to try to force your business through one particular strategic meat grinder. Instead I'm going to give you lots of little ideas and thought experiments which have the potential to reveal an effective strategy to you. Most of them will probably do nothing at this particular moment – other than perhaps fine-tuning your strategic brain – but a couple may give you a penny-dropping moment.

And that's all it takes really, a moment.

It's a bit like being lost in the woods. If I give you a map, but it's for a different location than the one you're in, then it will make you more lost. But if instead I teach you a selection of little navigation techniques that can be used in *any* scenario – like what side of a tree moss grows, or how to read the stars, or whatever – then one way or another you'll be able to find your way out.

This book is intended to be like that.

2. This book assumes you have a company already, but if you don't that's OK

As shall become clear, there are some fairly fundamental differences between formulating a strategy for an *existing* business, that's already been in the market a little while, and a *new* business, that's still in idea or startup phase.

In theory I could have written a book that covered both of these equally, but it would probably have been a bit confusing, so therefore I decided to write the whole thing as if you, the reader, already have a company to strategise with.

If you don't, it's not a big deal. The vast majority of the principles are equally valid to either scenario, and you can use your common sense as to what's relevant and what isn't.

The only thing I'd advise you to keep in mind, is that if you're developing a strategy for an as-yet-inexistent company, you'll almost certainly need to re-strategise and update it after you've been in the market a while, and seen how the world responds. It's extremely unlikely that a prototype pre-launch strategy will perform exactly as intended, so you should keep an open mind, and expect to continue refining it for a little while before you reach the "final" version.

For more established companies, the same thing doesn't apply. You should be shooting for strategic maturity with the ideas covered here – with the ultimate goal being the discovery of a direction that will work not only now but indefinitely into the future.

All good?

Right, let's get to it then.

What is strategy *really*?

OK, so we've already talked a little bit about what strategy isn't (i.e. bullshit), but we still haven't talked about what strategy *is*.

There's so much confusion floating around about this topic that I'm not going to assume *any* particular knowledge on the part of the reader here, and will instead strip things right back to nothing so we can build them up again.

For the purpose of this book, let's just pretend you've never even heard the word "strategy". Clear your mind. No preconceptions.

In that headspace? OK, let's start from the most basic place possible.

The "proper" but not very useful definition of strategy

In its purest sense strategy is simply:

> ***A plan designed to achieve a particular goal.***

Look up any definition you like and although you'll find different wording, you'll usually see something along those lines. If you want to

Understanding "value"

First, let's look at the *value* side of the equation.

The main way people screw this up is by confusing the value they provide with the *product or service* they make. If you ask someone what value their company delivers, they may respond with something like "we make cars", or "we provide legal advice", or "we run hotels". None of these are "value"; they are the *means* by which the business delivers value.

Value is instead the benefit that your consumer gets from your product. The thing they get from it which they "value" enough to choose it.

Let's think back to the IKEA example. If we say their value is to make having a stylish designer home accessible to everyone, then we can see that "flat-pack furniture" is simply a *tool* by which they achieve that. It's incidental. If they found another way of delivering that *same* value, but *without* flat-pack furniture, they could offer it and still be following the same strategy.

In fact that's just what they've done. They also offer homeware, as it stands to reason this is an important part of making a stylish home. Better still, they now even offer designer furniture tailored to disabled people – a move which makes perfect strategic sense if they are trying to make it accessible to everyone. Accessibility isn't only about cost.

See how everything hangs together under the central value offering?

A good way to visualise it is like this:

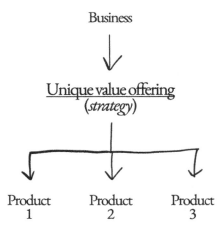

As you can see, the products are merely varying mechanisms of delivering the overarching value.

Make no mistake, the value is the thing the company makes, not the product. I'll repeat: your company is not your product; it's the value it delivers.

If you make the mistake of "product identification" and come to see your company as being synonymous with its product, rather than the value the product delivers, then you'll run into two issues:

1. You will struggle to create meaningful differentiation because most products are, by their nature, generic. All cars do the basic job of "being a car". It is only in the space of incremental value that similar brands are able to differentiate themselves.

The art ultimately – and the reason why it's not easy – is to come up with a value offering that is not only unique, but also desired / needed by a hell of a lot of people. Clearly this is tricky, because normally if there's something lots of people want, then there are already loads of brands offering it.

That's why good strategy is just so valuable. Finding something that loads of people want but which isn't already offered is like striking gold. You can't get it simply by asking people what they want – you'll never get a new answer there. You can only get it from lateral creative thinking – the kind of stuff we're going to focus on as we go through this book.

How strategy should shape a business

Hopefully now you get what unique value really means.

It means a benefit you deliver to your customers, *which they can't get anywhere else, which lots of them want or need, and which is big enough to animate an entire brand.*

Not too much to ask, is it?

Assuming that's all clear there is a final consideration you need to understand to have a true grasp of what strategy really is, and that is the way in which it *shapes the business which follows it.*

The core job of a strategy – any strategy, not just a value-based one – is to determine actions. To tell you what to do. It's a blueprint essentially, guiding you in your decision-making process.

In the case of a unique value strategy, its purpose is to help you mould your business into a unit which is exceptional at delivering that particular value to the market. Nothing more, nothing less. If it achieves this (and the strategy was decent in the first place) then the business will get traction and grow organically without you ever having to put in much effort.

(I like to say that strategy is an alternative to effort – both strategy and effort can get you what you want, but I know which I prefer.)

In order to understand how this shaping occurs in the most simple and intuitive way, I want you to internalise an idea I call "the strategic hierarchy":

The *Strategic* Hierarchy

Strategy
The unique value the business brings to the market

Delivery
The physical way the business delivers the value via product, behaviours, etc.

Branding
How the business communicates that value to the world in a clear and compelling way

This model, if you can call it that, sketches out the *entirety* of a strategically sound business.

At the top, you have the *strategy* – i.e. the unique value the business aims to deliver to the market; its existential core; its *telos* if you like; its *raison d'être.* Below this you have the *delivery* – i.e. the physical way the business actually does this via its products and services. And then finally you have the *brand* – i.e. the way the business presents and communicates this offering to the outside world.

(Some people would object to me reducing brand in this way, claiming that it's not merely about presentation and comms – and in a purist sense I'd agree with them. However, we have to work with the world as it is, and realistically this is the way people talk about branding now, so we've just got to roll with it.)

What you deliver. How you deliver it. How you communicate it. That's it! That's all a business need ever be, assuming it's strategically aligned.

Want an example? Let's take the good ol' chestnut that is Apple back in their Steve Jobs heyday.

Apple *Strategic* Hierarchy

Strategy
Computers which are friendly, intuitive, and accessible

Delivery
Cute, simple, toy-like devices such as the original colourful iMac

Branding
"Think Different", supported by advertising such as "Here's to the Crazy Ones"

As you can see, the big insight Jobs had was that rather than being these ugly, intimidating, nerdy things, computers could instead be friendly, fun, and easy for everyone to use – from a little kid to your granny. That was the essential value offering they wanted to bring to people; an offering which at the time was both desperately needed and truly unique.

The way they did this was to make cute, colourful, intuitive devices like the original iMac – which was *wildly* different from the average PC of the day. All their product decisions were oriented around the value offering – right down to putting a totally superfluous handle on top of the machine. You couldn't actually pick the thing up with it, and even if you could it would have been pointless since it wasn't portable – however, Jobs thought it made the device look less intimidating, so they stuck it on regardless. Strategic execution at its very finest.

Next, they had to communicate the offering in a way that would stick and give them ownership of that whole market space. Naturally they could have done something very direct and basic – "computers even your little sister could use!" – gauche stuff like that. But obviously branding is about communicating creatively, and often that means finding oblique ways to say what you mean. In Apple's case this gave rise to their whole "Think Different" schtick – which essentially meant being bold and imaginative, which the user-friendly design of their computers was meant to foster, and which stood against the grey mediocrity of their competitors.

Taken all together, these three elements added up to a strategically coherent whole – the results of which need no repetition.

Creating a business with a tight strategic hierarchy like this is the entire goal of what we're doing here. The strategy — the top bit — is an essential part of that, the point from which everything else flows, but it is *not* the goal. Having a strategically powerful company is the goal, and this is only achieved via the interaction of all three parts of the hierarchy.

Is there more to a successful business than this? Sure. But ultimately it's detail. If the strategic hierarchy is sound, it'll all fall into place without too much bother.

Offer compelling value to your customers.

Which lots of them want.

Which they can't get anywhere else.

Which your products deliver effectively.

And which your brand communicates memorably.

That's strategic mastery.

So how do we figure it out?

Coming up with an idea

It should go without saying that when you're coming up with your strategy, you can't simply do anything you want. You can't simply say "this would be cool", or "I'd like to do this", and make it so. Many founders do take this approach, of course, but it's closer to wishful thinking than strategy.

No, strategy is instead bounded by two things:

- The conditions of the market (i.e. the context in which you're operating)
- The nature of your business currently (i.e. the thing you're trying to guide)

An effective strategy emerges when these two things interact harmoniously; when the business "fits", just so, into market conditions.

This wouldn't be a strategy book without a Venn diagram, so I've illustrated this principle like so:

Strategy

Therefore, if you're going to come up with an effective value offering – one which responds to the realities of the market as it is, and which aligns with the nature of your business – you need to become an expert in interpreting both sides of the equation.

- What are the dynamics of this category and the other categories around it?
- What are the innate strengths and tendencies of my business?

(Clearly if you don't have a business currently then you would focus on the first of these, knowing that in principle you could develop an idea to match whatever opportunities you find – but as we shall see this is not really possible if your business is already operating.)

In this section then, before we come on to some tricks you can use to tease out potential strategic angles, I want to first talk about how we should read these two things. The underlying theory that links all great strategy, and the lens through which you should be looking.

First up...

How to read the market

The central idea I want you to have when thinking about the market is simply this:

Space It's an infinite open territory, where brands sit in different places depending on what value they offer. If two brands offer the same thing, they sit "on top of each other", resulting in a bloody and profit-sapping fight over who gets the spoils. By contrast if a brand sits alone then it has a relatively peaceful time – doing what it does for the people who need it, without too much threat from other parties.

Most energy in business is directed towards the first of those scenarios – "beating the other guy who's like you" – for the obvious reason that very few brands find themselves in the second scenario. We train ourselves and our teams to become "good at competing" or "good at fighting" because this is how we get ahead in the absence of strategy.

However, our goal here is to forget all that, and to put ourselves in the second scenario, that of a brand that sits alone. That's why we come up with a strategy in the first place.

You see, great strategies do not produce companies that are

"more competitive" or "better" than their competitors. That only applies when you occupy the same market space. Instead great strategies produce companies which have *no direct competitors at all*. Which don't have to play that game full stop.

This then is the mindset we should adopt when reading the market. Not one of competition, but rather *non-competition* – where our goal is to open up space, rather than to close it.

Now this may sound simple enough, but for most business leaders it's actually deeply counter-intuitive, because it cuts directly against their natural competitive instincts.

It means they have to abandon their understanding of business as a battle between companies, where the goal is to "beat" the other guy and steal their market share. And it means they have to stop trying to outperform them – whether that's with new features, better marketing, lower costs, or any of the other tools in the competitive arsenal. This competitive approach achieves the *opposite* of what we want to do here; it *closes* space rather than opening it, with the competing businesses gradually become more and more alike. When one goes left the other goes left; when one goes right the other goes right. They match each other's innovations, they match each other's prices, they refuse to allow the other to claim an advantage, until by and by they're basically interchangeable for consumers – "sitting on top of one another" in the market.

We commonly refer to this situation as "commodification", but I prefer to think of as "clustering", because it emphasises the irresistible way businesses in a market typically drift together over time.

Clustering

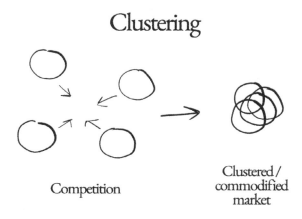

Competition

Clustered /
commodified
market

The perils of clustering are obvious and well documented. In short, because all the businesses in the market are offering the same sort of value, the only way they can gain advantage over one another is to cut costs and increase spend – i.e. hammering their profit margin.

You can see now why I'm so against the concept of being "better". Trying to be better rather than different *encourages* clustering and ultimately leads you (and your competitors) into a pretty unhealthy place.

A famous example of a heavily clustered (i.e. commodified) market like this was the US airline industry back in the '90s. Because all the carriers had realised the most lucrative customers were business travellers, they had gone to war in an attempt to be seen as the "best" for that market. This saw them gather into the same space and ultimately made the industry the least profitable in the entire country.

In fact by the mid-2000s *all* of the major carriers had at some point gone bust.

So much for being "competitive", right?

When we adopt a *non-competitive* mindset, however, where we seek to break away from our competitors, rather than going toe-to-toe with them, the opposite effect occurs: *declustering*.

Declustering

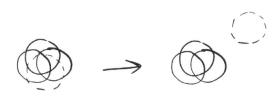

As you can see from the diagram, declustering means allowing your competitors to continue fighting over their favoured market space (i.e. their favoured value offering), while you go and offer something new.

In the case of the airline industry, this is just what Southwest Airlines did – choosing to forget about business travellers altogether and instead focusing their value offering on low-cost travellers. Executionally this meant doing away with business class, having no lounges, and flying on unfavoured routes. The result, naturally, was massive success – unlike every other brand in their industry at the time.

Notice how explicitly *non-competitive* this move was. It wasn't simply that Southwest decided to "add an offering" to their service – the way that many competitively minded businesses will when trying to steal a march on their enemies. No, what they did was far more powerful: they chose to *abandon* the popular market offering altogether, regardless of how "profitable" it supposedly was.

Southwest didn't care that *literally all the other airlines* were better for business travel than they were. They were totally cool with it. They knew that if they were going to bring a new value offering to the table they'd have to let that particular one slide, and this was a sacrifice they were willing to make.

I'm sure you've heard people say something along the lines of "strategy is about deciding what *not* to do", and this is a variant of that. We'll talk more about the power of sacrificing market position later on, but for now let it suffice to say that you simply need to stop looking at things through a competitive lens. Stop thinking of your competitors as things to "beat", and start thinking of them as things to manoeuvre around and *complement*.

A nice way to visualise this is to imagine the market not as a battleground but as an ecosystem.

In an ecosystem different organisms don't "compete" with each other, trying to drive the others to extinction. Instead they work *together*, symbiotically, to create a healthy overall system. They each have a particular "job" to do, and those jobs complement the jobs of the others around them.

By the same token, in a healthy market each brand does a *discrete* and *complementary* job to the other brands around it. This one looks after X, this one looks after Y, this one looks after Z, and competition never really comes into it. They each thrive in their own space and are cool with the others thriving too. Taken as a whole, they reach a state of *balance*, where everyone can grow and thrive without the profit-sapping annoyances of direct competition.

If you want to visualise this in its most extreme form, the perfect market would look something like this:

"Perfect Market"

This is what would happen if, say, the only car brands in the world were Jeep, Ferrari, Rolls-Royce, and Skoda. Perfectly differentiated brands doing discrete, complementary jobs.

Naturally this could never happen in the real world since the competitive urge will always arise, but you get the point. A great strategy can, however, create this situation *for you* – if not your competitors.

With me on all that?

OK, now let's look at how your company in particular might fit into it.

How to read your company

You now understand that the goal with our strategic hypothesis is to come up with an offering which moves us away from the other brands around us.

For ease of understanding, we can visualise this condition like so:

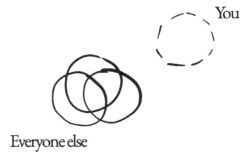

Pretty straightforward – however, it is at this point that we need to acknowledge that there are two ways a business can *arrive* at such a position, depending on what kind of company it is:

- Is it a company that "weirds the normal"?
- Or is a company that "normalises the weird"?

This is a crucial distinction which you need to get straight in your head before moving forwards, because knowing which type you are can have a profound effect on how you arrive at a strategy.

Allow me to explain.

Weirding the normal

For the vast majority of companies, strategy involves "weirding the normal", by which I mean taking a product or service that people are already familiar with and twisting it, so it becomes something new and exciting, and thus opens up fresh market space.

People knew what coffee shops were already, but Starbucks did it a bit differently. People knew what furniture was already, but IKEA did it a bit differently. People knew what airlines were already, but Southwest did it a bit differently. In all these cases the business was starting from a *generic category*, and then sought to bring a new value offering into the space. In other words they took something "normal" and made it "weird".

We can visual this motion as follows, starting "inside" the normal, familiar category, and pushing "out":

"Weirding the normal"
motion

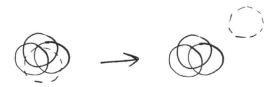

It's very likely that this is the game you need to play. Assuming that what you make belongs to a generic, well-recognised, well-established category (cars, funeral services, socks, cereal, gyms, laundry detergent, etc.), then your job is simply to find a way to make it seem fresh and different. To decluster the market in question.

The reaction you're going for is something like:

"I thought I knew X, but wow, this is totally different."

There's little more to be said about "weirding the normal", since that's probably what you've had in mind all along as we've been talking here. If you're one of them, you can skip ahead. However, not all businesses are in that position. Some need to do the opposite...

Normalising the weird

Occasionally you get brands who have a product or service which is entirely original and new. Something which isn't familiar to the majority of their target consumers. Something which confuses people – where perhaps they don't know what it does, why they need it, or who it's for.

For example I had one client here in the UK who made "juice shots" – i.e. small, concentrated juices featuring a hero active ingredient like ginger or turmeric. This was a confusing product. Most people had never seen something like this so didn't really know what to make of it. It didn't sit neatly in an established category like the brands we've talked about so far. If anything it established its own category.

For businesses like this, the strategic imperative isn't to "weird the normal", since they're already weird. Too weird, in fact, because people don't know what they're about. Instead the imperative is to *normalise the weird*: to take their strange new thing, and make it seem safe and familiar.

Now you might think that brands like this have it easy, because they are already doing something unique from the get-go. Isn't their unique value offering automatically inherent in what they do?

Unfortunately not. You see, *all* brands need to have some sort of grounding in a territory consumers already understand in order to be buyable. All brands need to be linked to some sort of mental category to make themselves understood. An unusual brand like this doesn't have that and might be able to frame itself around a dozen different potential value offerings, only one of which might resonate with consumers clearly enough to make it work.

As such, the job for inherently unique "normalising the weird" brands is not to push away from a category norm (since they don't start there) but rather to push *into* one, like this:

"Normalising the weird"
motion

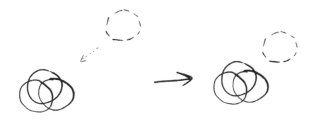

As you can see, the *end point* is identical for all brands – a position we might call "familiar but different": the strategic sweet spot. The only difference is the path they take to get there.

But how can a "normalising the weird" brand push into a category when it doesn't even have one in the first place? Well, that's the strategic decision, and comes down to the value you want to offer. Such brands will be able to deliver different value depending on the context in which you place them.

With the juice shot brand I mentioned, the most obvious category for them to enter was juice, since that's what the product was made of. However, in that category, they had very little leverage – they were basically a small version of the other brands around them; who would want that? The way they unlocked proper unique value was to move away from there and to frame themselves against a different category – that of sports drinks and supplements. In that space the product made much more sense, essentially as a fresh and natural alternative to the status quo. In order to execute that strategy, they needed to do various things which "tied" them to the new space (e.g. branding themselves in a manner that fit it more than juices), thus giving consumers a familiar reference point.

Do you see how by taking the same product, but aligning it with a different category, new value was created?

That's what normalising the weird brands need to do: push themselves towards a pre-existing space, with well-established norms, where what they do makes sense.

Finding the strategy you already have

OK, with that distinction out of the way, let's get into the weeds and take a real good look at the business we have – because you can bet your bottom dollar that the answer is hiding somewhere within it.

As mentioned earlier it's not enough to simply become expert at reading where market opportunities might lie, and what might be a promising strategy for some business or other. No, instead we need to be figuring out what's a promising strategy for *our* business – and that's likely to be very different from everyone else's. We aren't just trying to find open market space; we're trying to find open market space that's especially suited to us. Or, alternatively:

We're trying to find unique characteristics of our business which have the potential to create open market space if we push them hard enough.

I would argue that pretty much any vaguely successful business has such characteristics buried somewhere within it. Indeed it is probably these characteristics that have driven its success up to this point. If it didn't have them, it would have probably just failed. Trust me, they're there. The problem is that *founders are almost never aware of what these characteristics actually are*.

Your job is to discover them, match them to a market opportunity, and then – boom – you've got a killer strategy on your hands.

I often refer to this idea as "The Dolly Principle" in honour of Dolly Parton, who summed it up with the phrase:

"Find out who you are and do it on purpose."

There is so much strategic wisdom in this phrase. More than I've ever read in a strategy textbook, I can tell you that. Notice what she said here. She didn't say, "Decide who you *want* to be, and start doing it." She said, "Find out who you *are*" – meaning that you don't really have a choice in the matter; you are who you are and you simply need to embrace it if you want to go far.

By exactly the same token, your business, I'm sorry to tell you, "is what it is". Once you've launched it, it takes on a mind of its own which is totally separate from your preferences as a founder. The market interprets it in a way that suits consumers' needs and starts to pull it in that direction. You can't drag it somewhere else. All you can do is get in line with what it "wants to be" and help it accelerate in that direction.

This diagram will help you visualise this:

Founding point

Imagined path

What you think you've created

Actual path

What you've actually created

As you can see, whatever your initial idea on paper happened to be, it's almost certain that reality will have taken what you made and reinterpreted it in an unpredictable manner. You can tell this is true simply by the fact that things didn't pan out exactly as you expected them to. Perhaps one of your products failed, and another one succeeded. Perhaps the target audience you wanted to serve rejected you, and an unintended one embraced you. Perhaps you perform better in one kind of channel than another, despite putting equal effort into both.

All of these are signals from the market, and from your company, as to *what your company should become*. What people want from it. Where it has leverage.

You just need to let go of your original vision for the company, figure out what you've *really* created, and get behind it.

If you do this well, you'll find that you don't actually need to think of your business and the market as two separate things which you need to "match". Instead you just need to identify the things about your business that the market is favouring. Those things already fit and

simply need to be codified as a strategy you can execute going forwards
– i.e. "do on purpose".

There are endless examples showing why this is the best way to
develop a strategy. In fact I'd go so far as to say *all* strategically coherent
businesses did it this way. They begin with an un-strategic "prototype"
product or service, let it loose in the market for a while, watch to see
how it evolves organically, and then get behind whatever direction it
naturally drifts in.

Basically like this:

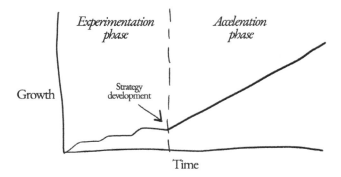

A classic example can be seen in the evolution of Facebook.

As most people know, Mark Zuckerberg never intended to create
anything like what Facebook has become. Heck, he didn't even intend

to create a social network. Instead his initial "vision" was simply to make a website where Harvard students could vote on the relative hotness of their classmates. By and by the site evolved, with Zuck cannily observing the way people were using it, until he realised that he'd actually created something very different – and far better – than his original intention. Rather than sticking his heels in and insisting on the sanctity of his "hot-or-not" concept, he got on board with what Facebook "wanted to be", and the rest is history.

To some degree or other this is how all effective strategies *must* emerge. They cannot be "imposed" on the business. They must instead be drawn out of it, by taking its strongest and most unique tendencies, and nurturing them.

If you simply develop a strategy "out of thin air", without observing the tendencies of your business as it is, even if the idea is *brilliant* in the abstract it will probably fail because it won't match the company you have. In my experience you cannot really "change" a business from one thing to another; all you can really do is focus and intensify it in the direction it's already leaning. Trying to totally transform something will probably kill it – not to mention chucking away all the equity and experience you've built up so far.

At the end of the day when it comes down to you versus your business, it's like a man trying to pull an elephant: you can't win.

So recognise that our job here is not to "create" a strategy, but rather to *find* a strategy that is already latent in our business as it is today.

Returning to our trusty diagram, it might help to think of it a bit like this:

Leaning into
a *tendency*

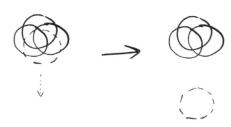

Here we have a business that has a bit of a "tendency" in a certain market direction relative to its competitors, and so in order to develop a strategy it simply embraced it and pushed it further – again, "doing it on purpose".

Don't get me wrong, the process is unlikely to be as linear as this diagram suggests; I'm simply illustrating that there is latent strategic potential in *every* half-decent business, and your job is to find it and accentuate it.

(If, however, you have a business that totally sucks and is failing every which way then you should be open to the possibility that you have nothing of strategic worth on your hands – in which case all bets are off!)

Don't fall into the trap of the self-loathing business

One possibility that occasionally trips founders up is that they don't particularly *like* the thing that their business is becoming. Perhaps they had a sexy or idealistic vision for what they wanted to create, and yet their business is pulling them down a more pragmatic path that doesn't match their dreams.

I call such businesses "self-loathing", for the obvious reason that they don't like what they are (or rather their management team doesn't).

I can recall one very big brand I worked with who had this problem *hard*. To the outside world, they seemed to have it all – huge profitability, a market space they totally owned, and a value offering that was crystal-clear to consumers (although never codified internally). However, I guess the people running the show got kind of bored of doing the same thing over and over again (operating a successful business is quite tedious unfortunately), and so instead tried to transition the brand into something they thought was more groovy and progressive.

Millions of pounds and a huge amount of effort later, they'd pretty much achieved nothing other than confusing and alienating a decent chunk of their core consumers. Quietly they shelved the plans and went back to being themselves. In the battle of company versus management, company wins every time.

What these guys missed – along with every other self-loathing brand – is that there is no such thing as a "desirable" or "undesirable" market position. What makes something exciting or not is how you execute it, and how much you commit to it. Does Ryanair have a sexy aspirational strategy? Not at all. But they have fun with it and execute with balls, which ultimately creates a charismatic enterprise.

Dull brands are those which are timid in execution and try to spread themselves too thinly over multiple market positions. However, if you attack your strategy with no apologies and no compromise, I guarantee you'll end up with something awesome on your hands.

And it'll definitely be better than the half-baked idea you started out with.

The three ways to discover the hidden strategy in your business

OK, let's recap what we've learned in this section.

1. The goal with our strategy is step away from our competitors and to create fresh market space
2. We must do this by leveraging existing characteristics hidden in our business
3. When we find those tendencies which connect with the needs of the market, we have the raw material for our strategy

Now is the time to actually do the work.

I'm not going to waste any time talking about research or data here. We should take it as read that in order to do this job effectively, you need to know a lot about your brand and its market (or potential markets). If you have reams of high-quality market research then that's great; it's good grist to the mill. But if you don't, I frankly don't think it matters hugely. You can be highly knowledgeable about your situation without having all the numbers at your fingertips. In fact, most of the really useful evidence you need doesn't come in the form of "data" at all; instead it's things like:

- The actions you've taken which have been surprisingly successful
- The actions you've taken which have failed
- The inherent qualities of your product relative to those of your competitors
- The inherent weaknesses of your product relative to your competitors
- A helicopter vision of the market landscape
- An understanding of your adjacent markets
- An understanding of the norms of your category
- Etc.

The list is limitless obviously, the point being that the highest-quality knowledge comes from *observation*, not number-crunching. You can never "research your way to a strategy"; the point will always come where you have to take a step back and look at the whole picture – a job which only human intuition can accomplish. Human intuition manipulating the raw material of holistic knowledge.

Assuming then that you have this knowledge at your disposal –

or are surrounded by people who have it collectively – you can start searching for strategic angles within it.

Here I'm going to lay out three ways of looking at things which may help you achieve this, all with the goal of uncovering the unique value you could offer.

Method 1 – Context shift

The beauty of this method, assuming it's an option for you, is that it allows you unlock massive value without necessarily changing anything about your product at all.

Instead, all you have to do is *frame* it against a different category, or set of competitors, than you are doing currently.

Value, you see, is totally contextual. An identical brand has the potential to perform entirely differently in two different environments. This is because the brand's *relative* merits will be different compared to a different set of competitors, and because different strengths will come to the fore depending on what the consumer is looking for in that particular moment.

We already touched on this briefly when I told you about the juice shot brand. When operating within the juice category, they didn't have much to offer, since they didn't really do anything that a juice shopper would be looking for. However, when framed in the performance drinks category, the same product had lots to offer, since the active ingredients delivered a "performance" result, but more importantly did so in an entirely fresh, healthy, and natural way. Because that category contained exclusively unhealthy artificial brands, the product had leverage there that it simply didn't have in the juice space. Thus, by shifting categories, they were instantly imbued with a powerful value offering.

I had another scenario like this with a client who made cereal bars.

When they launched 20 years ago, they were among the healthiest snack bars you could get, playing a crucial role in forming that now-massive category. However, as time moved on and health standards shifted, they gradually found themselves getting less and less healthy compared to the brands around them, until they became one of the *least* healthy bars on a shelf where health was the central competitive value.

Therefore, rather than doing the competitive thing, which would have been to tinker with the products to try and make them conform more closely to category expectations, we instead decided to abandon the category altogether and move somewhere where the current brand had natural leverage: confectionery (or candy bars for my American readers).

You see, although the product was unhealthy compared to the health bar category, it was still relatively healthy compared to regular candy bars. Not only that, in its new category the product's high sugar content became a strength rather than a weakness, because it allowed it to match the taste expectations that a candy consumer had – only with a much more "permissible" product.

In essence we had shifted it to become "the unhealthy person's health food" – something which may not have been healthy in an absolute sense but was a darn sight more healthy than the brands it was positioned with.

As a result the brand was then able to thrive in "dirty" channels where health bars normally don't do well, like corner shops and vending machines, giving it reasonably uncontested space to play in – *all without really having to change a thing about the product itself.*

To me it makes sense to always begin your analysis with the context shift, because it is probably the fastest and easiest way to discover unique value. It doesn't necessarily mean you won't have to change *anything* about what you do. Clearly your distribution, your targeting, and your brand may have to change. But it's still relatively simple and painless as these things go.

So how do you know where to look for an alternative category? It all comes down to identifying your *true competitor*.

The true competitor

The true competitor of Harley Davidson is not Yamaha, BMW, or any other motorcycle brand; it's a conservatory.

Can't remember where I heard this, but it's always stuck with me as a great way of explaining the concept of the true competitor. Rather than assuming – as most brands do – that your competitors are other brands that *look like you*, or that make the same kind of product as you, you instead need to shift your perspective to see your competitors as other things people might buy *instead of you*.

Often you will find, as with the Harley example, that these are wildly outside your direct category.

If you think back to Southwest Airlines and put yourself in their shoes, you might have reasonably concluded that passengers were choosing their travel options not only from among the airlines but from buses too. Makes sense, right? In that respect then buses were just as much of a competitor to Southwest as the other airlines were. Now clearly an airline has a *massive* advantage over buses in the speed and comfort of the journey, so if Southwest were to shift themselves into that part of the market, they would gain instant leverage. All they needed to do was take the necessary steps to ensure that they weren't too much more expensive: just enough to be justifiable given the extra speed. An airline who only thought they were competing against other airlines may never have thought of this.

Most brands have lateral, unexpected competitors like this. Competitors against whom they'd have massive advantages if they just framed themselves that way.

By drawing themselves in the direction of that unexpected category, brands profit on two counts:

1. They gradually differentiate themselves from their "obvious" category, and yet...
2. Will also never truly match their "new" category, and so will wind up in the uncontested market space we are seeking, just like this:

Framing against a
non-obvious category

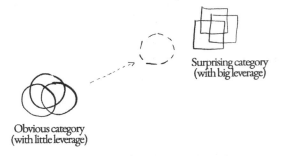

Surprising category
(with big leverage)

Obvious category
(with little leverage)

How do you figure out your true competitors then?

It's simple. You just have to understand the different motivations for buying your product (the different *value* it offers to different people) and then consider what other options they might have for satisfying those needs. Then, from those options, you can consider what your relative advantages over each of them are, to see if any would warrant moving in that direction for a more direct attack.

It's worth remembering that these alternative competitors may not necessarily be other brands. They could also be "non-brand" solutions as well. The true competitor of a bar is not necessarily another bar; it's someone staying home and watching TV. The true competitor of a Starbucks, as we saw, wasn't necessarily other coffee shops; it was the office. Ultimately the true competitor is *anything* that will steal attention from you and make you lose a sale.

The lesson here when you get down to it is that this notion of "category" is actually false and arbitrary. We invent this idea to make our lives easier, but in truth the world isn't mapped like that, and consumers don't think like that. The real world is far more messy. We imagine that people buy things by starting with a category need ("I need to buy some toothpaste") and then secondarily choose a brand from within that category. Whilst this is sometimes how it works (especially for un-strategic commodified brands), it's just as common for people to arrive at purchase decisions without even considering the other options of the category – particularly with strategically powerful brands.

Does the average Tesla customer go shopping for an electric car, or shopping for a Tesla? Does the average Patagonia customer go shopping for an outdoor jacket, or a Patagonia jacket? Does the average Harley customer go shopping for a motorbike, or shopping for a Harley?

You get my point.

Understanding that consumer motivations are far more complex than product categories make them appear has the potential to open up a whole new world of value offerings for you. Ones which other brands in your category would never have dreamt of, because they're so busy tending to the category-specific ways people arrive at them.

So bottom line, when a brand from an "outside" category starts to deliver the expected value offering of *another* category, it will automatically find itself in fresh market space. It will automatically be doing something unique, and it will automatically have leverage that the other brands in that space don't have, simply because they are so different physically!

You just have to figure out where the story makes sense.

Method 2 – Unexpected value

I began with context shift because it's one of the most rapid "hacks" you can use for developing a strategy – however, it isn't the most obvious.

That title goes to this second method, "unexpected value" – i.e. bringing a value offering to the category which has never been seen before and which goes against expectations. We might even call it "surprise value".

On the face of things this approach is pretty basic. Essentially it boils down to asking:

"What is a form of value that would make sense in this category, but which nobody has ever thought of delivering before because it seemed irrelevant?"

Basic, yes, but also quite difficult because it requires us to break with deeply ingrained thought patterns. How so? Well, all established categories have certain "core" value offerings within them that are so baked into our consciousness that it's hard to envisage anything else mattering in those spaces.

Examples of deeply rooted core value offerings like this include stuff like:

- Laundry detergent should be good at getting things clean
- Restaurants should have good food
- Computers should be powerful
- Clothes should be stylish
- Phone networks should have good coverage
- Etc.

These kinds of things represent the "norms" of these categories, and the territories that brands within them generally compete over. They are important, of course (nobody wants a phone network with terrible coverage), but they aren't strategically rich because everybody's into them, and therefore building an offering around them only serves to cluster the category.

Delivering unexpected value involves stepping outside of these assumptions and imagining what else this category could possibly be about.

Imagine, for instance, if we were to swap some of these value offerings around and move them into categories where they don't "belong". Surprisingly it creates some interesting opportunities. For example, we all know that cleaning products should clean well – that's a given. But what if they were stylish too?

Random as that sounds, that's just how the brand Method managed to cut through that particularly category. They noticed that cleaning products like bleach, degreasers, kitchen sprays, and the like were universally sold in ugly, brash packaging – in an attempt to communicate their "extreme" cleaning power (i.e. the category norm). This meant that consumers generally hid them away out of sight, under the sink. This is very different from food products like olive oil that are generally in very attractive packaging, inviting you to put them on display for everyone to see.

As a result Method thought, "What if we put cleaning products in beautiful packaging too?" The idea worked on a number of levels. Not only did it give them massive standout, since they looked unlike any of their competitors; it also accentuated their environmental credentials (another category norm), since the elegant packaging suggested a more gentle and higher-quality product.

This is a textbook example of unexpected value. Of looking past the locked-in assumptions of what a category is all about and exploring whether it could be about other things too.

There was no "rule" that all cleaning products had to be brash and ugly. There is no logical reason that things had to be that way. People just acted like they did. The category was caught in a habit. And when a habit like that takes hold, it creates strategic opportunity for anyone insightful enough to see past it.

I recently noticed a very similar strategy to Method's with the accountancy software brand Xero. They too, realising that they exist in a very clunky, functional, unsexy category, decided to try and inject a bit of glamour by positioning their software as being elegant and beautiful – summarised by their tagline "beautiful business".

In both cases, by using remarkably similar value offerings, the businesses found a way to get people to see their tired, dusty industries in a totally fresh way – precisely the potential of this approach.

Doing unexpected value right

What's important to note about both this and Method's strategy is that although the value they pursued was *unexpected*, it wasn't *random*.

You can't just bring any old value to any category. It has to have at least *some* relevance. It has to bring something to consumers that they actually *want* in that context.

In the cases of both Method and Xero, you can see that their offerings in some way accentuated core elements of their categories. For Method, in addition to improving shelf standout (which for any supermarket product is essential), the strategy also deepened their eco-cred. And for Xero, their strategy indirectly supported the more fundamental category values of simplicity and minimising admin fuss.

We're talking novel here, not nonsensical.

In order to strike this fine balance yourself, you might want to try exploring two questions one after another. First, ask:

What is our category *not*?

What things would you *never* really associate with the stuff that you and your competitors (or true competitors...) do? It shouldn't be too hard to come up with some stuff, because most categories are deeply entrenched in predictable norms, leaving a lot of territories totally unexplored.

Then, when you've thought of something, you must also ask:

Why?

Why does this value not exist in this category? Does it simply not make sense? Would it be unattractive in some way? Or would it be perfectly sensible, and its absence is nothing more than a failure of imagination?

Assuming you can't see any reason why not, then you can begin to explore whether the value has the potential to open up a lucrative new market space – and, just as importantly, *whether it's right for you*; whether there's something about your business that makes it the natural one to take this leap.

Remember our rule: unless your business is pre-launch or

totally failing, we are not trying to come up with an idea totally out of the blue here. We are instead trying to find a strategic path which would be a natural fit for *your* business to follow, based on its current characteristics and market performance.

Because of this, in addition to the theoretical thinking mentioned above, you should also be looking for the unexpected value that is lying dormant within your business itself.

What do you offer now, even if inadvertently or only slightly, which is unexpected or weird in the category?

Whatever it is, it's probably very subtle and largely accidental, but usually there's something there – especially in businesses that are doing well. There will be something that the market has picked up on and is enjoying which you haven't quite perceived. If you can tease something out like this, then – hey presto – that's the basis of your strategy right there.

I'll give you an example of this thought process, culminating in an unexpected value strategy.

For the first few years of their existence Airbnb was a product without a strategy. They knew what they sold and they knew people liked it, but they didn't quite know *why* people liked it – and so had no way of knowing how to forge a path forward in the market. Was the product popular because it was *cheaper* than hotels? Was their offering an economy-focused one? Probably not, since hostels were even cheaper. Was it to do with the social side of travelling? Did their leverage come from people being able to meet and hang out with their hosts? Maybe a bit, but lots of their guests stayed in empty properties too.

In the end they realised that their trump card wasn't any of this stuff – it was instead the feeling of *belonging*, the feeling of "not being a tourist", that bound their consumers together.

After all, the whole point of a normal hotel is, in a sense, to "incubate" you from the outside world. To separate you from your destination, and make things feel comfortable and predictable. When you go and stay in someone's house, however, like on Airbnb, that layer of protection is removed; you're right in the thick of things.

For a modern traveller, who didn't want to be seen as an old-fashioned map-and-camera tourist, this feeling of authenticity and connection was highly appealing – and thus the perfect territory around which to build Airbnb's strategy (which was ultimately summed up in their tagline, "belong anywhere").

Do you see how their unexpected value (belonging) was extracted directly from the business itself, and the way that the market responded to it? And do you also see how it was historically quite a weird thing for a hospitality business to offer?

It's a textbook strategic discovery process. They didn't "invent" the value; they *observed* it, ticking along quietly in their own business.

They asked:

1. What are we doing that's both unexpected *and* working?
2. How can we capture that?
3. How can we double down on it?

Or, more simply, they took Dolly Parton's advice – and ended up with something very powerful because it aligned with the principles of unexpected value.

Method 3 – Contrarian value

We might say that when we introduce unexpected value to a category, we are breaking "invisible rules", rules which everyone else in the category follows without even realising they're doing it.

That's all well and good, but what if we were to take things a step further, and break rules which weren't invisible, but *explicit*?

This is what contrarian value is all about. Here, we aren't saying "look at this new thing I'm offering". Instead we're saying:

"Everyone in this category thinks X, but we think Y."

It's strategy structured as a direct disagreement with the brands around you.

The key difference between unexpected value and contrarian value is that contrarian value demands that you actually *stop* offering something the category normally values, so you can unlock a new value that's incompatible with it.

A basic example: the console wars between Sony, Microsoft, and Nintendo have been waged largely on the basis of performance. Which machine is quicker, has the better graphics, and so forth. As a result we could say that power is a core value of the category, one which you'd seemingly be stupid to neglect.

However, that's just what Nintendo did. Realising that they couldn't beat Sony and Microsoft on the conventional performance metrics, they decided to go the other way and drastically *underperform* instead. By doing this they were able to produce a considerably smaller and lighter machine – so much so that it could be played not only on a TV (like Sony and Microsoft's devices) but also on the move as a handheld console with built-in screen.

The Nintendo Switch went on to become the biggest-selling console in the world – outselling both Sony's PlayStation and Microsoft's Xbox – ironically by being *bad* at the very thing they cared about.

This is contrarian value. When you decide to attack or neglect something in the category that everyone else cares about and in doing so unlock new territory.

What's particularly cool about this approach is that unlike unexpected value, it's almost impossible for your competitors to copy. I mean, let's face it, any cleaning brand could develop packaging just as nice as Method's without too much bother – and many have. Why not? It doesn't hurt them. It's not incompatible with their own offerings in any particular way. However, when it comes to contrarian value, the same thing doesn't apply, because in order to copy your offering, your competitors would have to *undermine* their own.

Southwest, who we talked about earlier, are also an example of contrarian value. Think about the dynamics there. They were only able to do what they did by *sacrificing* business travellers – the very bread and butter of their competitors. You couldn't service both audiences adequately no matter how much you wanted to. You had to make a choice. So could American and United follow them? No way. At least not quickly, and not without screwing themselves over even more than they already had.

To me, contrarian value is simply the best form of strategy. It not only creates unique and defensible positions; it also furnishes punchy and provocative brands, brands that have a real sense of fun and energy about them. It is also the most truly non-competitive of the strategy approaches. Although context shift and unexpected value do decluster the market in various ways, they both have a bit of "one-upmanship" about them. Contrarian value, on the other hand, is what truly decouples brands from a competitive context.

So why doesn't everyone do it? Because it's so difficult, of course. It requires going against our instincts in two big ways.

1. Contrarian value means willingly sacrificing market share

Central to contrarian value is a willingness to simply give your competitors big chunks of the market totally unopposed. You must be clear not only on what you offer but what you *don't offer* too. You must be able to say:

"Look, at the end of the day a lot of consumers are looking for X, and we simply don't do that – so they'd be better off going to our competitors."

Moreover, you must *respect* your competitors, by being honest about what they are genuinely good at, and what you're going to let them have. If you don't do this, then you'll always cling to the illusion that you can have your market space and theirs too – and so will never make the sacrifices necessary to deliver truly contrarian value.

This greed for market share is what kills so many brands – established and unestablished alike. One of the great cautionary tales here is that of Nokia: once the biggest phone brand the world has ever known, and now extinct.

Back when they were successful, Nokia dominated the market position for robust, cheap, everyman phones. They didn't *realise* this was their position, of course, because it was so frigging huge that it appeared to them that they simply dominated the phone market in general. What put things into relief, however, was the emergence of the iPhone – a product which represented the polar opposite value offering in every way: fragile, elegant, luxury.

The smart thing for Nokia to do in this scenario would have been to double down. To become even more tough and accessible in order to act as a compelling market counterpoint to Apple. The yang to their yin.

But, of course, this isn't what they did.

Instead, believing that they had a right to all segments of the market (as market leaders tend to do), they rapidly pivoted – transforming their products into inferior copies of the iPhone, and in doing so totally abandoning the market space people knew and loved them for.

Naturally this was a disaster, as they failed to put a dent in Apple *and* lost what they had all in one swoop – pretty impressive really. To this day nobody has really picked up the mantle dropped by Nokia, and probably nobody ever will.

Nokia's problem was that they didn't realise they had a strong contrarian value strategy right in the palm of their hand – all they needed to do was resist the temptation to attack Apple in Apple's backyard, and instead step away and follow a different path. However, this would have meant *knowingly sacrificing market share* – something they were plainly not prepared to do.

Apple, on the other hand, didn't give a damn for market share. Indeed for many years they never got above about 15% – nothing compared to Nokia's historic high of 50%. However, this didn't do their growth and profitability any harm, since that meagre 15% market share translated to a whopping 79% profit share. In other words 79 cents of every dollar of profit in the phone industry was taken by Apple.

This shows the profound power of contrarian value.

By abandoning large but highly contested market space, and settling instead for small but uncontested space (which, crucially, other brands can't readily enter), you create the conditions for massive profitability. A "walled garden" of your very own right in the middle of a raging battlefield. Who cares if you never dominate the whole market? That's not the game here. The game is to create a business which is effortlessly healthy and profitable. And this is achieved by surrendering space, not attacking it.

2. Contrarian value means actively cultivating weaknesses

The other counter-intuitive thing about developing contrarian value is that it involves not only accepting your weaknesses but nurturing them.

Most of us are trained through our careers to be "problem solvers": to keep an eye out for things that are wrong, for weaknesses in the system, and to address them when they arise. Although this can be pretty useful, it isn't much good for developing contrarian strategy, since it makes us interpret our weaknesses as problems, rather than the hidden strengths they really are.

When developing a contrarian value proposition, a good place to start is by identifying the areas you underperform in currently and then exploring what it would mean if you were to

underperform *even more*. What if you were to deliberately suck at them? What would happen then? What opportunities would that open up?

To show you just how far you can take this idea, look at the weird case of the Savannah Bananas, a minor league baseball team in the USA. The Bananas took the hugely unorthodox step of deciding to neglect the seemingly non-negotiable core of their whole industry: being good at baseball. What they did instead was to remove budget from the playing side of the business and invest it in the fan experience – making them by far the most entertaining team to go watch live (even if their on-field performance was pretty lousy).

From a commercial point of view this strategy had an obvious upside via increasing the gate receipts and thus the profitability of the organisation. After all, many people would rather watch a fun-but-bad sports team than a good-but-boring one. More surprisingly, however, the strategy also resulted in an improvement in their baseball results too – since they found themselves with so much extra cash that they were able to plough it back into the team after all.

The Bananas show us that there is perhaps no weakness which – when viewed strategically – doesn't contain an opportunity within it.

Ultimately this approach relies on the simple truth that you can't be all things to all people.

In order to effectively offer one thing, you have to be bad at offering another. Businesses who refuse to accept this, and try to cover all their bases, ultimately end up producing generic products and brands which consumers treat as commodities. Businesses who accept it, however, are able to create unique offerings which a portion of the market go crazy for – even if perhaps the majority aren't into it.

We can boil it down to this nice simple formula:

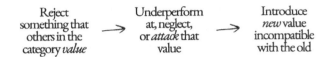

Reject something that others in the category *value* → Underperform at, neglect, or *attack* that value → Introduce *new* value incompatible with the old

So let's be real here, you're probably not very good at a couple of things your competitors excel at. There are probably a couple of areas where, if you're honest, other brands put you in the shade. If so, *good* – take those weaknesses and use them, because they are just the sort of clues you need if you're going to uncover a contrarian value offering.

Working this stuff through

We've given a lot of thought here to the theory behind teasing out a strategy, but I think it's important to spare a moment to talk about the *practice* of it as well.

Although you could happily sit in a room with this book and a pen and paper and try to "work it out" through brute intellectual force, that's not the approach I'd recommend. Instead I encourage you to make use of what is unquestionably the number-one tool at any strategist's disposal:

The humble chat

Yes, the chat – preferably one-on-one, informal, and open-ended.

Many people underestimate the power of the chat thanks to its loose, everyday, and "unprofessional" nature. They prefer instead analysis, workshops, number-crunching, exercises, etc. But whilst these often have their place, to me, they are all basically corporate pastiches of the chat. Flawed attempts to add veneers of respectability and science to the real sauce.

Chatting through a problem with someone supercharges your thinking. It is not simply a question of "doubling the amount of information" at your disposal because there are two of you. It's more like squaring it because the interpersonal dynamic adds new dimensions which you can't achieve in other contexts.

Consider the following qualities of a chat and how they might be useful to our enquiry here:

1. Chats are opinion-based

In strategy we are looking for opinions, not facts. Why? Because while facts are dull, one-dimensional, lifeless things, opinions are more concerned with the way facts *interact*. The space between the facts, if you like. And that's where insight is to be found. Thus you want to be exploring these questions in an environment where opinions are encouraged, and there's none more opinionated than the (possibly caffeine- or alcohol-fuelled) chat.

2. Chats are candid

The workplace (and indeed wider world) is of course ridden with hidden political pressures, expectations, and codes of conduct. As a result, anything with a whiff of formality about it is likely to become sanitised and diluted to the point of uselessness. Nobody wants to risk the kind of controversial thinking that actually makes change happen. In a chat, however (especially out of office hours), these restrictions are removed. Granted, it's hard to remove them completely if, say, you're the boss speaking to an employee. But even so, taking things "off-record" can be powerful in any context.

3. Chats pressure people to perform

Although chats are low pressure in terms of their atmosphere, they are high pressure in another way, and that is pressure to contribute. When there are only two of you there's no hiding. The silence must be filled. This of course is a big part of the way talking therapy works. When you're exposed and forced to talk about yourself, with no way of wriggling out, interesting things will eventually bubble to the surface. With chats, we can play the same game in a business context and unearth deeply buried information that may otherwise remain hidden.

4. Chats have room to breathe

Finally, a crucial way this underrated strategy tool differs from its more structured brethren is that it isn't tightly kept on topic. Chats are free-wheeling, perhaps without a well-defined start or a clean and tidy end. They have the capacity for tangents, small talk, gossip, and frankly totally off-topic lines of enquiry which are all useful to let the brain explore. Granted, this can make them pretty inefficient – lots of red herrings, blind alleys, and rabbit holes. But it also makes them surprising, and surprise is the very essence of strategy.

Considering all this, you can see why I suggest you develop your thinking in this forum.

Perhaps you might want to have the same chat with lots of different people, to see the different ways it might go. Perhaps you might want to arrive at some conclusions yourself, and then use some chats to test them. Or perhaps you might want to take one of the specific topics described in this book and make that the subject of the chat.

All in all, it doesn't really matter; there isn't only one way to do it. What matters is simply that you find a way of injecting a degree of opinion and informality into the process and prevent it from becoming too "rigorous" or "corporate".

I can tell you that the "secret" to my consultancy work, such as it is, is simply to first internalise the principles we've talked about in this book (so I'm thinking in the right way), and then just to chat to people who know a thing or two about the topic. That's it really. That's how 75%+ of the strategies are born – they just naturally emerge under that process of enquiry.

So let's not get too professional about this stuff, OK? Save that for the detail-driven drudgery of the day-to-day. Strategy's not like that. Like any creative endeavour it needs a bit of fun added to the mix. And a good chat will do that nicely.

Turning an idea into a strategy

So let's say you've got an idea. Or at least a thought. Who knows, maybe even two or three of them. Do you have a strategy?

No. Not yet.

You see the intellectual content of a strategy – the thinking behind it – is only half the battle. The other half is converting that thinking into a strategy that's actually usable.

It should go without saying, but a strategy is only as good as it is useful. Useful strategies have the power to:

- Align the whole business under a single coherent direction
- Provoke new ideas and initiatives pretty much instantaneously
- And most importantly, be understood by absolutely everyone

It's a funny thing, but I'd say that most "bad strategies" aren't bad because they are "wrong" or based on faulty assumptions. No, they are bad because they aren't even strategies in the first place. They are formulated wrongly. They don't do the jobs that a strategy should – and so even though they might have some brilliant thinking behind them, they are ultimately totally impotent. In fact I'd even take things a step further:

Bad thinking that's been crafted into a usable strategy is better than good thinking that hasn't.

At least with the badly thought through strategy you'll have something that provokes action, galvanises the team, and injects energy and purpose into the business. The market may well reinterpret it for you anyway, and make it work in spite of itself. The well thought through but badly crafted strategy, however? Well, at best that just does nothing – and at worst it sows confusion.

What we're going to do in this section then is take your thinking and put it through a series of tests, designed to engineer out the most common errors which threaten to make a strategy not a strategy.

It's kind of like that (surely apocryphal) tale of what Michelangelo said about carving David:

"It's easy, I simply remove the bits that don't look like David."

Well, by the same token we're going remove the bits that don't look like strategy, starting with the most fundamental one of them all...

The first goal of strategy

Strategy, as we've established, is all about difference. About the path that you're choosing to take which is different from everyone else's.

That much is clear, right?

Considering this, you'd be forgiven for thinking that the first and most fundamental goal of strategy is to simply create that difference between you and your competitors. That's what it's all about, surely.

Not quite.

I would say that making you different from your competitors is the *second* goal of strategy. The first is even more essential:

Making you different from yourself.

What do I mean by this?

Well, if you've decided to develop a strategy I assume your intention is to improve your situation. If everything is already perfect, then why bother? Clearly, however, in order to improve your situation, you're going to have to change some things about the company – your behaviours, your products, your brand – who knows? If you don't change anything, then you can hardly expect your situation to change either, can you?

That's why a strategy must, above all else, force you to change in some way from what you are today.

Your business must be obviously and markedly different in some way *post-strategy* to what it was *pre-strategy*. You need to see the fingerprints of the strategy somewhere on the business, in some crucial change which, hopefully, will be the trigger for growth and success.

Therefore, when you're looking at your strategy, the first question you must ask before anything else is:

Do we have to change in an obvious way in order to execute this strategy?

If the answer is anything other than an unequivocal "yes, duh", then guess what, you aren't just looking at a bad strategy – you're not even looking at a strategy at all.

Now you might be thinking, how is this possible? How could

someone fall into such an elementary trap? It's actually pretty easy –
and there are two ways it typically occurs:

Error 1 – Vague, wooly, "pretty" strategies

In some (or if we're honest *many*) cases, the reason a strategy doesn't
demand change from a business is because it's written in such a loose
and broad way that there are no obvious actions which fall out of it. It's
not that there aren't necessarily any changes that can be made, it's just
that they don't hit you in the face.

This is a particular risk if you try to write a "pretty" strategy.
You've got to remember, we're a long way off copywriting yet.
Nowhere in this book so far have I mentioned anything about trying
to write something that sounds good – but for many people (*especially*
marketing people) this is almost irresistible! Forget that. This is an
internal thing; it doesn't need to sound nice or elegant; it needs to
sound *specific* and *unambiguous*.

Pretty strategies are incapable of doing this because generally the
more creative and clever copy becomes, the more vague it becomes
too. Imagine say a brand whose strategy is something like "inspire
the incredible in the everyday". I just made this up, but I dare say all
of us have come across something pretty similar at least once in our
careers. Probably more than once actually. There are loads of problems
with this sentence, but first and foremost is the issue of *what the hell
do I actually do with it*? Does it tell me anything? Does it give me an
instruction? Does it demand anything specific of the business? No,
clearly not – so we'd be hard pressed to identify an obvious change we
need to make.

By contrast, let's think back to IKEA, who essentially have a strategy of "making designer interiors accessible to everyone regardless of wealth or background". (These aren't literally the words they use – that's not public info – I'm just illustrating a point here.) What does this strategy immediately demand of the business?

1. We're talking interiors, not just furniture, so they need a homewares division as well
2. The key attribute of the products is to be designer, so they must invest heavily in that, always keeping on top of trends and churning out new designs regularly
3. The products must be cheap, therefore they must leverage innovative cost-saving mechanisms like flat-pack and out-of-town retail environments
4. The products must be widely available
5. The products must take account of different living conditions people might have, for example being very low on space, having kids, having limited storage, or being disabled (all of which IKEA cater for)

Probably I'm a bit off on some of the details here but that's not the point. The point is that there are some super obvious *demands* being made by the strategy here, which, if the business were to ignore them, would totally undermine it.

Now ironically IKEA's *tagline* is very similar to our fake pretty strategy written above – "The wonderful everyday". And that is fine, because it is a tagline designed for broad communication, not a strategy.

You can see, however, how an "ugly but specific" strategy can evolve into an "elegant but vague" tagline – so don't get ahead of yourself; that will come. For now just keep it clunky.

Error 2 – Strategies which you are magically somehow following already

This second error may be an issue with the strategy, but it also may be an issue with the founder's *interpretation* of the strategy.

Essentially this boils down to you saying, "You know what, I think basically we're already doing a pretty good job of this," and thus weaselling out of having to make any uncomfortable / expensive changes.

If you feel this way, there are two possibilities:

a) You're right: you are already following the strategy perfectly, in which case it must be pretty poor if you're not getting the results you want

b) You're rationalising, and coming up with clever arguments to convince yourself you're doing something you're not

In the case of this second one, there's a pretty easy way to tell if you really are following the strategy already. Just ask:

Would an external observer (like a consumer) agree with you?

Would a punter be able to "see your strategy" in the business just by looking at it? Remember, we're dealing in *value-based strategies* here, so they are not secret or hidden within the bowels of the business;

they should be coming to life externally, out in the market. They should be blatant.

The reason people love to use the big iconic brands as case studies in their business books is because you can see their strategy from the outside. You don't need to have secret internal knowledge. Apple, Red Bull, Patagonia, IKEA, Tesla, etc. – I talk about these brands so I don't have to bore you with 10 pages of background waffle to make a simple point, because I know you know all about them already. Any idiot could have a decent stab at explaining precisely what they offer to the market.

This then is what you should be shooting for too – external obviousness. "Wearing your strategy on your sleeve". Remember it is not only the responsibility of the branding and marketing departments to tell people what you're doing (that's a bonus) – instead they should be able to intuit it by simple observation, without any messaging at all. Do Tesla tell you what their game is explicitly in their marketing comms? No, they don't even do marketing comms. They don't need to. They are sufficiently strategically aligned that it's obvious; people get it.

So yes, although I appreciate you might have a very good and sophisticated argument for why what you're doing now is, in fact, "actually" on-strategy, if you're having to make the case then you've already lost. It must be totally obvious without explanation.

As you can see then, it's quite possible for a strategic thought to stumble at the first hurdle. It's not the strategy that's actually going to get you results – that's just some words on a piece of paper, or in a PowerPoint – it's the actions the strategy provokes. The *changes* that will make you different tomorrow from how you were yesterday. They need to be big, binary, and in your face if you want to get results that are like that too.

You with me?

Right, that's one challenge sorted, let's get ready for the next one – because it's where even more people fall.

The subjectivity test

This is quite a subtle point, so rather than confuse you with preamble I'm just going to come out and say it:

You must remove all subjective language from your strategy and see what's left.

What is subjective language? Anything that's in the eye of the beholder, anything that's a judgement, words like:

- Good
- Great
- Incredible
- World-class
- Best
- Smart
- Etc.

Words like these are often inserted into strategies as "filler" to disguise the absence of a strong thought or insight. The reason we remove them is because it reveals if there's any underlying *substance* to the strategy; if there's anything left over when the hyperbole is taken away. If you find it impossible to write or explain your strategy without resorting to subjective language like this then – you guessed it – you don't have a strategy!

But why, you may be wondering, can't I construct a strategy using words like these?

Two reasons:

Reason 1 – Subjective language isn't specific or directional

The job of a strategy is to tell you what to do. To give you an actionable plan. Subjective words like this don't do that – instead they simply state the desired *reaction* to what you do. Both the Ritz and your local B&B might offer "outstanding service", but clearly they are wildly different businesses with very little strategic overlap. The word "outstanding" therefore tells you *nothing* about what specifically these businesses are doing to create leverage in their markets, and as such it may as well not be there at all. It doesn't serve a purpose beyond sketching a vague aspiration.

Reason 2 – Subjective language is a sign of a dreaded "better" strategy

Whenever a subjective word crops up, you can bet your bottom dollar that it's disguising a "better" strategy like we talked about earlier in the book. When all is said and done, it probably boils down to a strategy of "be better than the other guy", and as such it opens no fresh market space, and thus isn't suitable for our purposes.

I mean, think about it. Whenever you're forced to qualify what you're doing as being "good" or "great" or "excellent", you are basically saying that all your competitors do this thing too; they just do it a bit worse. If, on the other hand, the thing was new, and your competitors weren't doing it, there would be no need to qualify it, would there? You could just say it straight, without resorting to "salesy" language to puff it up and make it sound like more than it really is.

Ultimately what you need to understand here is that subjective judgements about whether something is "good or bad", "smart or dumb", or anything like that, *do not belong to you*. They belong to the market. They belong to your customers.

Your job isn't to be "good". Your job is to offer something *specific* which some people will think is good, and some people will probably think is bad.

Even if you have a passionate aspiration to excel at some generic value offering in your category – and you're *convinced* that by doing so you'll gain market leverage – it still isn't enough to say that's your strategy. You need to explain *how* you're going to excel at that thing. That's your strategy. For instance, a yoghurt brand couldn't blithely state "our strategy is to have the best-tasting yoghurt". What does that even mean? But they could say "our strategy is to replicate the flavours and codes of ice cream in yoghurt". Ah, OK, that's an actual idea. And yes, it would be interpreted by many people as being "the best-tasting yoghurt". But here you have an actual objective strategic rationale as to why this would be the case.

(NB I'm not proposing that this is a good strategy – I'm simply saying that it is a strategy, unlike being the "best-tasting".)

Anyway, I could go on, but let's not get bogged down by theory. Simply let it suffice to say that good strategies can be written in totally objective and sober ways. They don't *have* to be (you could probably "jazz up" a good strategy with some pointless verbiage if you wanted to), but they at least *can* be.

The subjectivity test is designed to push your strategy into that shape. And in addition to weeding out any non-strategies that may be lurking, I think you'll also find that it makes things a hell of a lot clearer too.

The opposites game

I'm only going to touch on this technique briefly, because it has a fairly similar rationale to the subjectivity test, just looked at from a different angle.

Essentially the idea of the opposites game is to ask the following question:

Would the opposite of this strategy also make logical sense?

If the answer is yes, then you've probably got a pretty good strategy on your hands. If the answer is no, then maybe not.

The reason this question is powerful is because good value-based strategies are meant to offer consumers strong alternatives to other legitimate offers in the market. For a basic example, let's say that you decided to be the low-cost option in your category. Totally legitimate and sensible. Now what's the opposite of that? Being the premium option, of course. Also totally legitimate and sensible. In either case you would be offering something that it would be rational for your competitors *not to offer*, and thus you'd be opening space.

Imagine, on the other hand, that you were a law firm with the strategy of winning the most cases you can. As opposed to what? All your competitors who are trying to lose cases? It's nonsensical. Or how about a delivery company who builds its offering around punctuality? What's the opposite of that, all the delivery companies that are trying to be late?

I realise these sound stupid, but trust me, so many so-called strategies fail the opposites game. They fail to represent alternatives to other legitimate options which might be offered by other companies.

Remember, only strategies which your competitors might choose *not to do* are legitimate. Strategies which everyone would agree with, and which everyone would be keen to pursue, are illegitimate.

There is a variant of the opposites game which I sometimes use, but which is built on the same principle: who are you trying to alienate? Who are you trying to turn off? Who are you trying to push away?

We spend so much time thinking of the customers we are trying to attract that we often neglect the equally important question of who we are trying to repel. If you look at your strategy and can't think of anyone who would reject it, then, once again, you don't have a strategy on your hands.

When Tesla decided to build the electric car market by offering luxury performance cars, rather than cheap, economical little runarounds (which were the norm in that category at the time), they did something with a legitimate *opposite*; something that many electric car consumers would reject. This is why it worked.

Just like with the subjectivity test, the opposites game reveals strategies that are just glorified "better" strategies, only it does so by interrogating the idea in a different way.

If you pass both of them, then congratulations – I'm pretty sure you've dodged that fatal bullet.

The how cascade

OK, this is a good one, I think.

As I'm sure we all know, many brands get in trouble when they confuse goals for strategy. At its worst this manifests in dumb statements like "our strategy is to double our turnover" or "our strategy is to become number one in our category by 2030". I'd like to think that any reader of this book wouldn't do anything quite so heinous as that – but you never know, because I've seen plenty of billion-dollar blue chip corporations saying such stuff, so perhaps I overestimate people.

In any event, the rest of this book should have steered you away from abject nonsense like that – however, that doesn't mean you're safe from the goals-as-strategy trap altogether.

You see, there is a more subtle version of the crime that I myself have committed on numerous occasions, and which can be quite hard to spot even when it's staring you in the face. I call this a "goal/

strategy": something which isn't a pure goal (which should be easy to spot) but which also isn't really a fully functioning strategy either.

Let's look at a hypothetical example.

Say you worked for a dog food brand and decided that your strategy was to "become the number-one dog food for pensioners". What is this – a goal or a strategy?

On the one hand it does do something we expect of a good strategy, namely making a firm choice and narrowing your options. It's picked a specific audience – pensioners – and therefore has boxed all of your future decision-making into following that path. A pure goal, like "becoming number one by 2030" has no such decision within it. It's completely open.

Nevertheless, in spite of this strategy-like quality, we'd have to say that overall it's really still a goal. For one thing, it's very much an *aspiration*, rather than a *solution*. It states what you want to be rather than what you want to do. And for another, it fails to explain *how* you're going to achieve it. Yes, sure, we've narrowed our scope, but ultimately we're still left with more questions than answers. How exactly are we going to appeal to these pensioners? What are we going to offer them?

Trust me when I say that a lot of really good-looking strategies have this problem. They seem to be sufficient, they seem strategic, they seem to "do enough", but when you get down to it they're still just tarted-up goals, which ultimately leave you unsure of where to turn.

The how cascade is a tool you can use to resolve this issue – and make sure you don't accidentally move forwards with a goal / strategy.

The way it works is simple. To any strategic statement or idea you might have, ask this one word:

How?

How are you going to do that thing you're stating? When you've answered that, ask again. How? Keep asking how until your answer has the quality of a solution, rather than an aspiration.

Let me show you:

- We want to double our revenue by 2030
- OK, how?
- By becoming the number-one dog food for pensioners
- OK, how?
- By tailoring our offering to lap dogs, which they disproportionately own
- Ah, OK, got it

Do you see how after the second how we transitioned from an aspiration to a solution? From the vague to the specific? That's the point where a goal becomes a strategy.

Of course, you could have kept on asking how. But when you get "lower" than that you transition from the level of strategy to the level of execution, or tactics. In truth you can follow the how cascade all the way from the very loftiest ambition right down to the purchase of a single paper clip; that's how all-encompassing it is. The art is recognising which "slice" of the cascade represents strategy – and the answer is that it's the first layer where a solution is proposed, but *before* getting into executions of that solution.

Perhaps it would help to visualise the entire cascade like this:

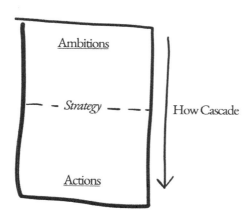

In my imaginary little example above, I use the phrase "ah, OK, got it" very deliberately – because that is the feeling that a fully baked strategy should provoke. A person should "get the gist" at that point and be able to start filling in some of the remaining blanks themselves. In the case of making a dog food for lap dogs, we can start to speculate pretty comfortably about what that might look like, or how we might go about doing it. That speculation is executional thinking – the thinking that should organically emerge from the strategy.

Unfortunately many strategies don't provoke a reaction of "got it" – instead they provoke reactions such as "OK, and what does that mean exactly?", or, of course, variations of the word "how?". Sometimes we might even say they leave people more confused than they were with no strategy at all.

Always keep in mind this is meant to be *helpful* to people. It's a *service* you're giving them, not a demonstration of your intelligence, passion, or ambition. And as with any service, the question "how?" should already be answered.

The toilet paper rule

The preceding ideas dealt with the *structural* issues a strategy might have, whereas this one is a bit more concerned with the content.

Naturally there are an unlimited number of reasons why a strategy (even a well-constructed strategy) might be "wrong", and so it would be pointless to start speculating on them here. Nevertheless I would say there are a couple of recurring errors that are worth addressing thanks to the frequency with which they arrive, and the toilet paper rule deals with one of them.

The crux here is recognising that different product categories have different levels of innate *interest*. Fashion? Interesting. Accountancy? Boring. Cars? Interesting. Bleach? Boring. Holidays? Interesting. Water softener salt? Boring. When a category is interesting consumers are prepared to devote a lot of time and energy into thinking about it, whilst when a category is boring they will tend to get "in and out" as quickly as possible, and not allow it to take up too much of their consciousness.

Now these varying "bandwidths" that people apply to different categories have a profound effect on what's going to fly at the strategic level. You see in a high-interest category, the consumer's attention and care enables brands to adopt quite sophisticated, rich, even lofty strategies. They'll be prepared to read, to research, to explore, and to an extent become immersed in the brand world. By contrast, in a low-interest category, brands have no such luxury – they need their offering to smack the consumer in face in half a second flat, to operate on an almost visceral level.

The reason I call this the toilet paper rule is because the brand Andrex is a good example of how to do it right from a low-interest position. What do Andrex "own" in the toilet paper category? Softness. That's what they're all about, and because they've been doing it for so long they've been able to claim ownership of this attribute even though it's such an obvious offering. How do they communicate that softness? No room for subtlety here: puppies. This is soft toilet paper sold to you by puppies. That's it.

This approach is strategically sound, but more importantly it's incredibly shallow and unsophisticated. This is what gives it its power, because Andrex knows that toilet paper is an extremely low-interest category, where consumers buy pretty much on zombie-auto-pilot, and don't have the time or inclination to swallow any grand offerings.

Compare that to brands like Lululemon or Patagonia, which have extremely rich and subtle brand worlds through which they artfully communicate their strategic angles, and you'll see the difference.

High-interest categories can support sophisticated value offerings. Low-interest categories can only support blunt value offerings.

To hammer the point home I've illustrated it in this highly scientific diagram.

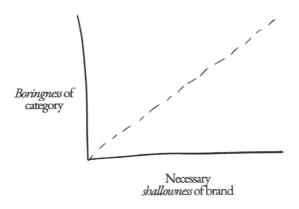

Boringness of category

Necessary shallowness of brand

The error then, clearly, is to try and laden a business in a low-interest category with an overly lofty strategy. Where you particularly see this occur is in the case of so-called "purposeful" brands, where the strategy is built on some sort of moral crusade. This may be all very nice, but I'm sorry, nobody is going to be lectured by their toothpaste on the plight of the rainforest. There's simply an *attention mismatch*, and your proselytising is going to fly over people's heads.

Frankly I feel sorry for low-interest brands – not because they have a difficult job on their hands (actually their job is arguably easier) but because the examples that are used in the business press are just so misleading for them. The sexy brands that everyone uses to explain their points (me included) are often sexy purely because of the category they occupy. Sure, Red Bull are awesome, but let's not forget they're an energy drink – something which is pretty cool from the get-go. Nike, yeah, wonderful brand and all that, but come on, they make athletic apparel – you'd struggle not to have a decent brand in that space.

I had to laugh when I was reading the book *Blue Ocean Strategy* (which is a great book, I hasten to add) and saw that they were using Cirque du Soleil as one of their case studies. I'm sorry, but a literal *circus*? If you can't build interest and exoticism into that then there's truly no hope for you. How is this meant to help the founder of a plumbing supplies merchant? Yes, the core dynamics are the same – but translating them across such a gaping interest divide requires a very sophisticated understanding.

What you need to understand is that although you can (and should) make your brand *relatively* interesting in comparison to alternative purchases, you can't make it interesting in an absolute sense. There will always be a locked-in level of "give a damn-ness" that you'll be carrying around with you, and you must work with that, rather than denying it.

Put simply: if people don't care about your category, don't try and make them.

Instead shoot for short, sharp, simple, black-and-white leverage. The sort of thing it would be impossible to miss, even if the consumer was only considering it for a couple of seconds (which, most likely, they are).

As for those of you in high-interest categories, well, the good news is that in principle "anything goes" in terms of sophistication (within reason, anyway – all strategies should be fundamentally simple). The downside for you is that you'll probably be playing in a far noisier and richer competitive environment, which makes standing out that little bit harder.

In either event, though, a crucial ingredient of any strategic value offering is a deep respect for the consumer – for their time, for their priorities, and even for their biases. What you think they "should" care about is nothing. What they do, in fact, care about is everything. So whatever you do, make sure you operate honestly and realistically within those boundaries.

The challenger trap

This final test concerns another common content error, like the toilet paper rule. And a pretty insidious one at that.

I'm sure that most of you have heard the term "challenger brand" before – essentially an upstart insurgent brand that challenges the orthodoxy of its category. Naturally a lot of the strategic techniques we've talked about here – particularly contrarian value – would help create challenger brands, so overall it's a concept I have a lot of time for. If you want to think of yourself as a challenger brand then that's great, crack on.

But you've got to be careful.

You see when people think about challenger brands, various iconic examples of the idea tend to spring to mind – Ben & Jerry's, Patagonia, The Body Shop, Innocent, etc. As a result, many people jump to the conclusion (quite understandably) that this is what challenger brands look like and behave like. Essentially they think, "If I want to create an awesome challenger brand like them, then I should learn from them and copy them."

Big mistake.

Although the great challengers were indeed challengers in the past, *they aren't challengers anymore*. They now represent the status quo. They're "the man". Yes, they still *talk* like they're challengers, and act like they're standing up for the little guy, but at this point that's little more than a stylistic hangover from their early days. The fact is, they are market leaders who set the norms of their category, rather than subverting them.

As a result if you copy such brands, or allow yourself to be overly influenced by them, you are actually doing the opposite of what a challenger should do. You are fitting right in with the status quo! You're attacking the market leaders with a set of values that the market leaders have already fully adopted.

To give you an example, think of the UK juice and smoothie brand Innocent. Arguably there is no brand that is more quintessentially "challenger" than them – they completely upended the grocery scene with a focus on health, simplicity, and ethics that the old-school legacy brands simply couldn't match. However, that was back in like 1999. Today, when Innocent are a Coca-Cola-owned corporate behemoth, those values are completely standard across the supermarket. Every big P&G, Unilever, and Pepsi brand makes a show of them because, thanks to Innocent and a few others, that is now what is expected by consumers. It's normal.

However, this doesn't stop new so-called "challengers" coming along on a daily basis acting as if a healthy / simple / ethical offering is somehow revolutionary and different. They have been seduced by the power of brands like Innocent into believing that "this is what challenger brands are about", but of course they're not. Challenger brands aren't about anything in particular at all – they're simply about something *different from the current prevailing orthodoxy.*

A challenger juice brand today would be *against* Innocent, not a disciple of it. A challenger ice-cream brand would be *against* Ben & Jerry's. A challenger outdoors brand would be *against* Patagonia.

Of course it's quite hard to do this because these "first-generation" challengers are so goody-two-shoes that it feels impossible to go against them without being "bad" – but that's not right. Nobody is saying that you can't also share some of their values – the point is simply that you mustn't expect those values to give you market leverage. At best they should be hygiene factors. "Yes, of course we are environmentally responsible, that goes without saying, but what we really want to talk to you about is X." You have to find a new territory of value. You have to change the terms of the conversation and move it into a territory where those brands are weak or have nothing to say.

Bottom line: don't try and fight the status quo with the status quo.

Sounds obvious when I put it like that, but thanks to the sheer cultural power of these brands it happens all the time.

The implication of this for your strategy then is simple. Just ask: am I doing something genuinely new here? Something genuinely "challenging"? Or am I actually fighting a straw man, attacking an enemy which old challengers defeated years ago but who they pretend still exists for their own marketing purposes?

Naturally it's totally contextual, but speaking broadly I'd be quite suspect these days of consumer brand offerings which are built on health, simplicity, the environment, or activism. I'm not saying you can't do these things. And I'm also not saying that you'll never find a powerful strategic angle within them. What I am saying is that they are where most people's heads are going first, so you'll have to be pretty artful (or lucky) to strike gold in such a heavily mined landscape.

(And by the way, don't play that game of saying, "Well, my competitors claim to be ethical but we're ACTUALLY ethical," or anything like that. That's a "better" strategy, as I'm sure you can spot by now. You need to change the conversation, not just push harder in the direction it's already going.)

Challengers challenge the status quo *today*. As it is right now. They do not set up an imaginary map of the market and challenge that, no matter how flattering and righteous it may feel.

Actually writing the strategy

We've got this far talking about a "strategy" as this sort of nebulous free-floating idea and haven't yet addressed what it actually is *physically*. What actually am I holding in my hands here? Is it a PowerPoint doc? A single sentence? A pyramid, an onion, or other such arbitrary shape?

Up to this point it should have sufficed simply for it to be a thought in your head, or series of rough notes, but now that we're getting close to the point of firming up the strategy for final use, we're going to need to make things a bit more formal.

And so I'm going to tell you exactly how I personally write a strategy for maximum usability.

Ditch the deck

If I had to guess, I'd say most strategies floating around out there exist in the format of "The Deck" – a nice long PowerPoint presentation, probably replete with a few pillars, onions, missions, visions, and the like.

This is a mistake – in fact, arguably one of the foundational mistakes which results in a strategy degrading to bullshit status.

Imagine, for a second, that you have a great strategy. It's tight, it's exciting, it's clever. Then imagine finding yourself in a bar, chatting to a prospective investor / employee / dating option, and the conversation gets around to it. How do you explain it to them?

First up, you're not whipping out a diagram. Any strategy that needs a drawing of some sort to explain it has already got some serious problems. And second, you're not going to spit a bunch of jargon or "copy" at them. You're a human trying to communicate with another human, after a couple of drinks, so there's no room for corporate spin here.

No, instead, you know what you do? You just explain it to them! You open your mouth, form some sentences, and try to string them together into a compelling argument, culminating in the punchline of what your strategy is.

That's all there is to it. So why in the business environment would things be any different?

Your job when putting a strategy to paper is simply to explain it so that anyone who reads it, gets it. And therefore all you have to do is write it the way you'd tell it – as a single page of A4, with a few paragraphs of argument and explanation, culminating in the punchline ("therefore we are going to do X").

This is a job for Word, not PowerPoint (or whatever your non-Microsoft Office alternative might be). Why? Primarily for the very simple reason that PowerPoint is designed as a *presentation aid*, which is meant to be accompanied by a human being talking it through.

Word, on the other hand, is designed to produce documents which are read, not presented, and therefore the information you put down in that format needs to stand on its own two feet. Thus, a strategy laid out as a single piece of flowing prose is far easier to share than one in deck form, which is always going to be incomplete and disconnected without someone there to talk it through.

There are other benefits to a prose-based strategy write-up:

1. Prose allows you to present your strategy as an argument

Although your strategy ultimately will culminate in a single sentence ("our strategy is to do X"), in order to give someone a real understanding of it you're going to need give them an explanation too. Any such explanation is invariably going to be structured as an *argument* for why this strategy might work. You're basically saying, "Because of this factor, this factor, and this factor, the smart thing for us to do as a business is X." You're also taking the opportunity to address any obvious concerns or counterpoints which might arise.

As a result, your strategy write-up should look something like a lawyer's closing argument in a trial. "Ladies and gentlemen of the jury, here are the facts, and that's why you must come to the conclusion that this strategy is indeed the correct one."

Written prose is a beautiful medium in which to make such a case, and it demands that you structure your points in a self-contained logical flow. In a deck – or God forbid, a framework – information can simply be "dumped" without explanation or connection. Such formats don't demand that you state your case. They don't hold your thinking to account. This is fine if you're simply mentioning the strategy to an audience who already understand it. Then you can use whatever shorthand version you like. But in the *master* strategy document – the one that ultimately every action in the business must refer back to – you must include the *argument* as well as the conclusion.

Another reason for this is:

2. Prose encourages people to internalise the strategy and repeat it in their own words

As you can imagine, one massive no-no with strategy is *memorisation*. If people are memorising your strategy like they're learning lines in a play, then you can be sure they don't understand it. And if they don't understand it, they can't execute it.

Writing a full and coherent argument diminishes the risk of memorisation for the pretty basic reason that it's just too damn long to do so – it's far easier to simply remember "the gist" of the argument, which in turn allows the reader to make it their own.

It's like if your pal tells you a funny story about a friend of theirs. When you come to tell it to someone else later, you're not going to repeat it word for word, are you? You couldn't even if you wanted to. Instead you'll take the essence – the bit that's easy to remember – and give it your own spin... perhaps even embellishing a little if the mood strikes.

We want people doing exactly the same thing with the strategy. Remembering not the words but the *story* of the words. And because a strong argument is a story – with a beginning, middle, and end – a write-up like this will do just that.

3. Prose will expose bad thinking

The final benefit of setting out your strategy like a little essay is that the format is just so unforgiving.

Let's face it, a PowerPoint lets you get away with all manner of bullshit that wouldn't fly in a conversation or email – that's why people love it so much, and why they constantly use it in lieu of a Word doc even when they're not planning on presenting anything. With straight-up prose, however, it's just your words, in black and white, having to hold people's attention and stand up to scrutiny all by themselves.

You might find when you come to actually write the strategy that the very act makes it fall apart. You'll spot holes or contradictions that you weren't aware of before, and you'll struggle to piece together an explanation that you'd feel comfortable sending to someone without you being there to defend it.

That's *good*. That's a key part of the process. Like so much of what we've talked about here, if you want to de-bullshittify your strategy you need to put it through such tests to establish whether it's truly worthy of dictating the entire future of your business. With such an outcome at stake, it's only reasonable, right?

Now you might be thinking, "But Alex, I'm not a good writer. How am I ever going to be able to convert my strategy into a clear, concise, and defensible essay?" If that's the case then I refer you to my earlier point about describing the strategy to someone in the pub. You may not be a good writer, but you can talk, can't you? You can string a couple of sentences together? That's all this is. In fact, that's all it ever should be. There should be *no difference* between your written explanation and your spoken one. If you find your writing style to be markedly different from your speaking style, then you're probably clouding your writing with layers of bullshit. Remember the old adage that writing is a service, not a performance. Heck, if it helps just record yourself explaining the strategy to someone and then write that up (with a few common-sense edits, of course). They'll probably help you by querying a couple of points too.

What structure should I use?

OK, so you get my point about laying out your strategy as a mini-essay on a single page of A4 – but within that, is there any further structure that might be useful?

Yes, there is, although I encourage you to take it with a bit of a pinch of salt.

What I normally do are four sections:

- Background
- Strategy argument
- Strategy summary
- Delivery

The core strategy argument will be less than a page, but the whole thing might run to two or three pages – don't worry about that. The only goal is to have a single written document which you could email to *anyone* and have them say, "OK, cool, I get what you're doing there."

I think those sections are pretty self-explanatory, but here are a few extra pointers with an example write-up for Tesla:

(NB in case not blatantly obvious please note that this is not Tesla's actual strategy write-up, and for all I know may not have even been their actual strategy. I've just made it up, using an example of a brand we're all familiar with. The point is not the content; the point is only to illustrate what a write-up might look like. Got that? Right, on we go.)

Background

To be safe, I suggest you assume your reader has never even heard of your company before and has no familiarity with your market. Thus a couple of sentences saying what the business is and a note on the relevant conditions of its market at the time of writing would probably be useful.

I like to write the whole strategy for the general man-on-the-street, which is easy with consumer products, but obviously if your business is in some really complex or specialist field don't bother describing it from scratch – in that scenario you can assume some prior knowledge.

So for Tesla back when it first launched it might have been something like:

"Tesla are an electric car startup with ambitions of transitioning the mainstream car consumer to all-electric power – and eventually doing the same thing for other areas of their lives through battery technology.

Currently, however, electric cars have a tiny market penetration,

generally being seen by ordinary drivers as inconvenient and
unattractive."

Strategy argument

Here is the meat of your case: the laying-out of the relevant facts, your insight into them, and the conclusion you've reached over how to move forward. Speaking broadly it's likely to take the format of first describing the status quo of the market, why you think that's lacking, and then what you're prepared to do in order to offer something different.

In the case of Tesla it might have been something like:

"The current paradox with the electric car market is that in addition to being green it is often positioned to consumers as being highly economical as well. This is reflected by the current cars on offer generally being tiny, dull, city runarounds – the most economical and 'sensible' offering possible.

However, this doesn't really stack up for two reasons. First, 'practical and economical cars' is an offering which appeals to consumers who aren't especially interested in cars in general, and so are barely even aware of the existence of electric cars at all. They are not early adopters. And second, even at a basic level the offer is a lie: electric cars aren't economical; they're expensive and hard to use, with much more in common with a luxury good.

It's our belief that if you wanted to give electric cars

mainstream traction, you would need to start from the top of the market (luxury performance) and work your way down, rather than starting at the bottom (economical little runaround) and working your way up.

In this manner you would be able to target wealthy status-conscious consumers who aren't concerned with cost and convenience, thus giving you initial market traction, AND you'd also set the electric car up as an exciting aspirational product for the mainstream consumer (to whom you could offer a cheaper model when sufficient interest had been built).

Therefore our strategy is..."

Strategy summary

Having made your case, you want to wrap it up with the actual core strategy itself – which should probably be a single sentence. Remember that this sentence is meant to be practical and explicit, *not pretty*. Don't worry about being elegant; worry about being clear. This might result in something quite clunky, but so long as people get it, don't worry.

A slight issue with this explicitness, of course, is that it can sometimes make the strategy cumbersome to refer to in subsequent conversations, so for that reason I also sometimes like to give the strategy a name by which people can refer to it in the shorthand. This name won't be self-explanatory, of course; it's simply for the use of people who already get it.

So for Tesla we might continue with:

"Therefore our strategy is as follows:

To establish electric cars as symbols of luxury and performance, rather than frugality and compromise.

*We call this **'the trickle-down strategy'.** "*

You might note here that I probably could have written this strategy with a dozen different wordings but all with the same meaning, and that's just what we want here, as that's what everyone will be doing. We want people to be able to articulate it their own way. Also note that the name I gave the strategy nods at how the strategy works in the market and provides additional information on top of the basic strategy sentence. That's not essential by any means but I think creates a good overall "package" in this case.

Delivery

Even a super-crisp strategy is still, ultimately, going to be fairly abstract, so it's important you really land the idea (and get the ball rolling) by listing some key actions arising from it.

What are you going to have to do in order to deliver on this? What needs to change? What do you need to stop doing? What needs to be added?

In principle this list of actions might be endless – after all, the greatest brands are marked out by the crazy lengths to which they take their execution, going far beyond what's necessary to simply be "on strategy". However, at this juncture I'd limit things to simply the key two or three points which are going to make the binary difference between doing the strategy and not doing it.

Generally you're going to want to divide them into different sub-sections, something like this:

> *"In order to deliver this strategy Tesla will have to execute in the following ways:*
>
> ***Product***
> *Our first car will be top of the market in terms of both performance and luxury – the Roadster sports car. We will follow this with an all-out luxury vehicle (the Model S), which will still have game-changing performance, before then dropping down into the more mainstream segments of the market.*
>
> *However, even at that point our cars will always be market-leading in terms of performance, technology, and design. No Tesla car will ever be mistakable for electric cars from the legacy brands.*
>
> *We will also reset the expectations consumers have over cars in a number of performance and luxury areas, including:*
>
> - *Never-before-seen levels of acceleration (as enabled by electric technology)*

- *Imaginative and fun car features (e.g. in-built video games)*
- *Use of the best modern technology (e.g. car run from app, self-driving tech, etc.)*

Distribution

Unlike other car brands Tesla will not sell through franchises but will instead run its own stores. This allows us to take full control of the customer experience and heighten the luxury experience of the brand.

Branding and design

Legacy car manufacturers all have a similar interpretation of 'luxury' in their branding and aesthetics, leading them to all be quite similar. Because we are representing electric power in the market (which the consumer considers to be 'high tech') we will bring a different version of luxury into the category: what we might call 'tech luxury' as pioneered by brands such as Apple. This means minimalism, bare wood, clean lines, limited use of words, and no superfluous details such as buttons, controls, etc.

This will enable us to stand out as a different kind of luxury in comparison to brands like Mercedes and BMW."

Obviously this is all speculation, but you can see how these elements – which are indeed true to Tesla in real life – stack up to my example strategy in a coherent and distinctive manner.

Knit that all together then and it's going to be a pretty good strategy – one which will be able to stand on its own two feet as the brand's "north star" for an indefinite period of time.

By now you should really be able to see how everything we explained earlier on in the strategic hierarchy knits together into one cohesive whole.

- Here's the situation
- Here's our reading of it
- Here's our idea
- Here's how we manifest that
- Here's how we package it

In other words an entire business, top to bottom, laid out in a few simple paragraphs.

Pretty neat, no? And, as I'm sure you appreciate, pretty rare too.

If you have something like this, well done. Enjoy it. Kick back. Bask in its glow. Because – after all that – you're now going to realise that all you've done so far is lay the groundwork. The real work begins now.

Executing a strategy

By now you're probably bored of me saying that the strategy is nothing and the strategic action is everything – but nevertheless I'm duty-bound to repeat it.

The action is everything.

It's the only reason you did the strategy in the first place. You're like a farmer who's spent months meticulously attending to his crops whilst everyone around him scattered seed at random – so it would be pretty perverse if now you refused to harvest them.

Hence we really need to dedicate a few pages to the subject of execution.

One of the most surprising realisations of my career is just how variable executional ability is across brands. In the past I was more than happy to simply look after the strategy, and then step away to let the brand get on with executing it alone. However, I would estimate that only maybe 40% of brands did what I'd call a "decent" job of executing – with perhaps 20 or 30% doing a downright terrible one.

Why?

There are a couple of reasons which spring to mind:

1. **Strategy execution is incremental to the day job**. Most of the activities you're gonna need to do to make a strategy happen need to be done *on top* of the normal running of the business; therefore you need a certain amount of "slack" so you can dedicate time to it. Any brand that is running flat out all the time – especially at a senior level – is going to come unstuck here because they simply won't have the capacity to make the strategy happen.

2. **Strategy execution only happens properly when the strategy has been fully internalised**. Even with the cleanest and most simple of strategies, it's going to take people (yourself included) a few weeks, or even months, to truly digest it so it becomes part of their natural "operating system". Until this happens, execution is always going to be a bit clunky and "forced" because it cuts against the old ways of thinking that are more deeply ingrained in the business. This can result in confused, contradictory thinking, and ultimately saps momentum from the project.

3. **Strategy execution gets killed by rationalisation**. As we touched on earlier, many businesses let themselves off the hook when it comes to execution by telling themselves they're doing it when really they aren't. Weirdly many seem to think that the mere existence of the strategy on paper magically equates to its existence in the real world

– "we have a strategy, therefore we are strategic". But obviously that's nonsense. You have to keep in mind that a strategy only exists if it can be perceived from the outside of the business, not the inside – and that takes a hell of a lot of commitment.

For these reasons I now try to stay involved through the implementation process far more than I used to, since ultimately outside perspective and accountability is the only way you can really "cure" these issues with any degree of certainty.

(I'd strongly encourage you to get someone – anyone, frankly – to act as an external observer while you execute, since otherwise the risks of you deluding yourself in some way are just far too great.)

Through this experience I've come up with a few concepts which I think are pretty much universally helpful in taking strategic action, so let's run through them now.

Minimum viable strategy

We've all heard of "minimum viable product" right? I.e. the most simple and easy-to-execute version of a product that still fundamentally works, with potential embellishments being for further down the line? Well, "minimum viable strategy" (MVS) is exactly the same, only with strategic actions.

What is the bare minimum you need to do in order to be genuinely following this strategy?

Typically (although, I stress, not always) this will probably be something like:

- Minor tweaks to existing product
- Introduction of / planning for new product
- Rebrand

The benefit to this way of thinking is obvious: it stops you biting off more than you can chew. It breaks what can be an overwhelming challenge down into something that should be pretty achievable in the space of 6–12 months. As always, your challenge to yourself should be *what do we need to do in order for people outside the business to understand what our strategy is?*

Remember throughout this whole book we have been talking about value-oriented strategies: strategies which shape the value you are bringing to the market. As such the strategy must be *perceivable* by the market, otherwise it may as well not exist at all. So most of your key executional actions are likely to be very externally visible.

Some brands try to get around this by essentially "telling" their strategy in their marketing comms, but not really delivering on it at a practical level. That game doesn't work. Marketing comms should always be seen as the cherry on the cake of your business, not the thing that drives it. A well-executed strategy can be perceived by the market with zero comms support – the comms simply hammer it home.

So another way of thinking about your MVS is: what is the minimum we need to do for consumers to understand our value offering without us telling them what it is?

If you can arrive at two or three ideas to achieve that, then you'll be in a really good spot – go out and do them.

One thing I should stress at this point is that although an MVS will probably only comprise a couple of actions, that doesn't mean that you should only come up with a couple of actions off the back of your strategy. A strong strategy should prompt a *deluge* of potential ideas and behaviours. You should be able to tell it to anyone and have them come up with a couple off the top of their head. If a strategy doesn't prompt ideas *automatically* then it has a problem – probably one of being too abstract, and not practically grounded enough. Your MVS ideas should be a *selection* from your ideas, not the only ideas you can think of. The ones you've identified as being foundational to your success. The others might well take you to another level, but they're not the immediate priority.

As an aside on this point, yet another advantage of MVS is that it can help focus that breed of founder who wants to do "too much" with their strategy.

As we'll come on to, I'm all for over-delivery of strategy providing that it's done in the right order. What isn't so good is executing a bunch of random stuff off the back of a strategy whilst neglecting the fundamentals that actually make it really work. For example, in the Tesla illustration we used in the last section, clearly launching an expensive sports car as their first model was far more foundational to their strategy than installing video games onto the car's entertainment system. Done this way round, everything makes sense, but if they'd done it the other way round, it would have just been a bit random and weird.

We're trying to create difference here, yes, but crucially it must be *coherent* difference. And that means "stacking" your strategic actions in order of priority: recognising what is a must, and what is simply a nice-to-have.

One way to think of this which may be helpful is to imagine the three following competing businesses:

Business A: 100% generic
Business B: 90% generic, 10% different
Business C: 30% generic, 70% different

Clearly business A isn't what we're shooting for, because it has no leverage. But we're also not shooting for being like business C either, because it's likely to be so unusual that consumers will struggle to be comfortable with it.

Business B, on the other hand, is probably that Goldilocks blend of "just right" – being overall quite familiar and easy to navigate, but with a couple of powerful strategic differences built in which allow it to create fresh market space.

Correct application of an MVS should allow you to hit this spot. Yes, we should aspire to be pushing things a bit further in the future – to 20%, even 30% different – but that's a luxury. Just crossing that binary divide from not executing your strategy to executing it is enough for now.

For me, I find a recurring theme in *all* strategic thinking is "big to small". Starting at the macro level and working your way down to the micro level in a sequential fashion. This applies to the relationship between strategy and strategic action ("big" strategy cascades down to "small" action), but it also applies *within* action itself ("big" foundational ideas precede "small" textural ideas).

Keep everything in that cascading order, and whatever you produce is bound to be deeply coherent – the essence of strategy.

Cross-category copying

Look, I always go into projects saying to clients that the strategy we come up with won't *necessarily* result in a rebrand. And technically it's true – you have no idea up front what actions a strategy is going to demand, and indeed I have worked on a couple of projects where no significant branding work actually took place.

However, being real between you and I... you're probably going to need to update your brand. New messaging, new aesthetic, new packaging, new creative expressions, all that stuff.

I mean, it stands to reason, right? Think back to our old friend the strategic hierarchy:

The *Strategic* Hierarchy

Strategy
The unique value the business brings to the market

Delivery
The physical way the business delivers the value via product, behaviours, etc.

Branding
How the business communicates that value to the world in a clear and compelling way

If the job of the branding is to communicate the unique value you're bringing to the market, then if you update that value, you're almost certainly going to need to update the branding.

Of course, given that we haven't plucked our strategy out of thin air, it's very likely that your existing branding will at least be obliquely communicating the strategy. But oblique isn't really what we're aiming for here – we want smack-you-around-the-head obvious. You can – and often should – retain the essence of your existing brand. But you're going to need to *intensify* it in the direction your strategy leads you.

Naturally the process of doing this is a pretty standard one, which anyone who's been through a branding project will be familiar with. The only difference is that unlike most branding projects, you'll be giving the creative agency a genuinely strong brief in the shape of your strategy document. You're basically saying to them, "This is what the business is – how should it present to the world?" They'll probably have never seen another brief like it – and like all narrow briefs, it should provoke great work.

However, there is one little extra idea I want to throw in on this subject, because I think it's quite cool and can sometimes be helpful to brands following bold strategies – and that is "cross-category copying".

Cross-category copying is where you copy elements of the branding of other brands with similar value offerings – providing they are in totally different categories.

Obviously there will be no brands in *your* category with the same value offering, because that's the entire point of what we've been doing here. However, it's likely there will be brands in entirely different categories who are delivering something vaguely similar, albeit under completely different circumstances.

The reason it makes sense to copy them, is because often they will have done the hard work of building mental shortcuts for consumers between their offering and a certain visual style. And if you adopt that same visual style, then you will be able to communicate your offering far more efficiently and intuitively.

I know that's a bit theoretical, so let me give you an example.

In the pizza category, the "aesthetic norm" is probably something like "old Italy". All swirly writing, leaning towers, and the implication that it's just like Mama used to make. This stands to reason, of course, because this is basically a way of communicating "nice pizza". However, one brand that did things entirely differently was Dominoes. Their branding, relatively speaking, is bold, simple, and even somewhat corporate. It's also clearly been incredibly successful. Why?

Well, if we think about Dominoes' value offering, particularly in the early days, we can see that it's not really focused on quality pizza but rather *efficient delivery*. They don't "own taste" (that's a generic category expectation, anyway); they own "getting it to you fast". Now who does this remind you of? Not any brand in the food space but rather delivery companies like FedEx and UPS. When we take a step back we can see that Dominoes are not branded like a pizza brand but like a delivery brand. They feel essentially like a competitor to FedEx – except, of course, they aren't; they are merely borrowing the credibility brands like that have built up in the delivery space.

As a result Dominoes are able to:

1. Look entirely different from their category
2. Communicate their value offering efficiently
3. Seem instantly familiar and "safe" to their customers

...all at the same time. Pretty good going, no?

Remember how I said our goal is to be "familiar but different"? Well, cross-category copying is a great way to build familiarity without resorting to looking like your competitors (generally a big no-no).

If you think I'm cherry-picking the one vaguely plausible example of this with Dominoes, consider these other cases:

- As we mentioned earlier, Tesla present themselves not like a car brand but like a tech brand in the Apple mould. This contributes to their offering and looks like the kind of thing their customers are already buying, just in a different space.

- The brand Vitaminwater made their labels look pretty explicitly like pill bottles you might be prescribed by a doctor, in order to land their slightly dubious "medicinal" offering, showing that you don't necessarily need to copy a *brand* to play this game – any aesthetic shortcut will do.

- By the same token the original iMac, which we also mentioned earlier, got across its message of childlike accessibility and friendliness by looking very much like a toy or even a piece of candy.

- And of course the cosmetics brand Lush lands their core "freshness" offering by styling their stores subtly like a fruit and veg market.

Naturally whatever you're copying needs to be intuitively understood by the market as representing that thing you're offering – you can't just find some random brand doing something similar and copy them, because the familiarity isn't there. But if you can find something everyone "gets" as being in the same territory then you'd be well advised to have a look at it.

This is all about that art of balancing difference with sameness, danger with safeness. We are trying to stand out as much as we can, whilst also "fitting in" – a paradox, I admit, but not an unachievable one.

As an aside I should note that there is one circumstance where you *would* copy your direct competitors, and that's if you're a brand who is "normalising the weird" as we discussed earlier. In those cases, where you're trying to take a unique product and "connect" it to a well-understood category, it's almost essential to copy the codes of that category in order to do so. You don't need to worry about the fact that you're going to "look the same", because all of your difference and leverage is going to take place on the product level. You're already weird, remember?

This is precisely what we did with that juice shot brand I mentioned. We tied it aesthetically to the norms of sports drinks like Powerade and Lucozade, knowing that they were so wildly different on the product level that the similarity could only help us, not hinder us.

All make sense?

I don't want to give the impression that you must do cross-category copying in order to be strategic. Often it's entirely unnecessary. It's just that it can be an effective way to bring things "back down to earth" if you're pursuing a truly bold and unique direction – which I hope you are.

We must never allow the desire to be different to drag us into overly niche or freakish territory. The market is at its heart deeply conservative, being driven far more by inertia than the search for novelty. This is especially true with lower-interest categories (see: toilet paper rule). So as ever respect the consumer, respect their time, and above all respect their deep ambivalence for whatever game you're playing. Only then will you be able to overcome it.

The creative canvas

Both the concepts of MVS and cross-category copying sit within what we might call the "baseline" of strategic execution. They pertain to big and important changes, sure, but ultimately they're also rather humble, since they seek only to make your business "on strategy" rather than "off". There is, however, another dimension to execution, which moves beyond simply "doing" the strategy, and into the territory of over-delivery and even *flair*.

You see, whilst strategy is binary (you're either following it or you're not), it's also on a spectrum, where some brands will go wayyy further than others in bringing it to life.

You know all those cliched case study brands everyone likes to talk about? Many of which we've mentioned in this book? What links them is not simply that they are strategic, but rather that they have all gone to extreme lengths in over-delivering on their strategic offering. This is what makes them charismatic, distinctive, and easy to talk about.

For example, Southwest Airlines could have followed their strategy simply by getting rid of business class seats and flying on less popular routes. It probably would have done the job. What they didn't need to do was to follow it *deeper*, by allowing their cabin crew to become overly jokey and familiar with their passengers. This element of their execution – which they are now famous for – was a completely *optional* manifestation of their strategy, which went well beyond MVS. But even so they did it anyway, elevating them to a higher level of market presence than a "merely strategic" brand could ever hope to achieve.

Patagonia are masters of creative over-delivery. At the strategic level, there isn't a huge amount there – especially nowadays, when environmental concerns have become a category generic in outdoor gear. Nevertheless, they manage to own this broad market territory completely, thanks largely to the sheer lengths to which they execute on it. For instance, as far as I'm aware they were the first major brand to make the commitment to repair all clothes bought from them forever, for free. They were also the first brand to sell their underwear loose, rather than in boxes. Retail experts told them this was suicide, but they did it anyway because it was demanded by their strategic promise to "cause no unnecessary harm". The boxes were unnecessary and harmful, so out they went – and surprise surprise, sales went *up*.

Even more so than Patagonia, Red Bull's very *business model* is an exercise in taking execution too far. Again, there's nothing particularly clever about an energy drink brand trying to own the market space of "pushing you to achieve awesome things" (which is essentially what the whole "give you wings" thing boils down to). Indeed I'd almost say it's strategically vacuous. However, when you push it so far that you essentially turn your little drinks company into a media empire with a drinks brand bolted onto the side of it, almost as an afterthought, then you've really done the strategy equivalent of turning water into wine. There are few brands so singular as Red Bull, despite its pretty basic underpinnings.

What all these brands show – whether we're talking at the level of little gimmicks, or total business transformation – is that pushing your strategy to its limits is wildly effective. And fun too.

So how do we do it?

The way I like to think about it is via the idea of "the creative canvas".

Basically if you take your average business, they tend to have this idea that they are "allowed" to be creative and adventurous in their branding and advertising, but not in the rest of the organisation. In other words their "canvas" for creative expression is something like:

- Visual identity
- Copy lines
- Advertising campaigns
- Social media platforms
- Website

Standard stuff. What the great strategic brands do, however, is to expand their creative canvas to incorporate their entire business. They take the same sort of imaginative thinking that most brands limit to their advertising, and apply it *everywhere*.

Naturally the specifics of this canvas will vary depending on the brand, but if we imagine, say, a gym chain it might include:

- Design of the space; how does our strategy demand this look?
- Choice of equipment; is there anything unexpected we should add, remove, or even invent?
- Staff profile; what sort of person should work here?
- Staff behaviour; how should they behave differently to other chains which would be on-strategy and memorable?
- Additional amenities; what should our gym offer outside of

fitness which no other chain has, and which would have an amplifying effect on our strategy?

- Locker rooms; how do we do this differently? Do we even have locker rooms?

(The women-only gym chain Curves famously did away with locker rooms altogether, partially in order to create a less intimidating environment, and partially to save costs and unlock new locations.)

I could go on, but you get the point. The entire business is a playground for creating strategy-enhancing experiences.

Note here the use of that word "enhancing". We aren't talking of changes that are essential to your strategy. They fit into the MVS bracket, and you just have to do them. They may be wild and revolutionary (heck, they *should* be), but they don't count as over-delivery, simply *delivery*. Where the fun starts is when you move to the next layer and explore the "optional extras".

Early on in my consultancy career I was particularly fascinated by the potential of this "embedded creativity" concept. It seemed weird to me that there was this whole industry dedicated to creativity within *media* (i.e. advertising), but there was no equivalent industry for creativity within the fabric of businesses themselves. This is especially true in the internet age, when word-of-mouth has become so crucial for promotional purposes. If you create a business which is anecdote-worthy, or "talkable", then the business essentially becomes its own walking ad. If people go on your airline, say, and something surprising happens, then they'll go away and talk about it. If, however, the whole experience is predictable then they won't. As a result my adage to people has always been to "make interesting companies, not interesting advertising". It's expert-level stuff, admittedly, in a world where so few brands are capable of mastering the strategic basics – but it's something we should shoot for, no question.

The creative canvas is a simple way of visualising just how vast your potential for performative strategic action really is. Simply step back and map out all the different territories and touchpoints that you might be able to twist into something more aligned with your strategy than the generic status quo. Then it's merely a question of trying to generate some ideas. You don't have to do it everywhere, of course – in most areas you'll probably find that the generic approach is the sensible one. But if you find one or two good 'uns... that's all you need to turn the gap between you and your competitors into a chasm.

The CPG dilemma

One limitation we should address with the creative canvas is just how variable it is depending on your industry. I mentioned airlines and gyms above because they have an unusually rich array of consumer touchpoints and moving parts, meaning that they have a huge creative canvas.

Many brands, however, don't have that luxury, especially your average CPG brand you'd find in the supermarket.

In those cases there is effectively only one moving part out there in the world: the product itself. And as a result the potential for incremental strategic execution is extremely limited.

The short advice I'd have for such brands is basically: don't worry about it. Just execute your strategy to the MVS level and you'll probably be fine. However, there are a couple of other levels that might be worth exploring:

- **Format and packaging innovation**. Aligning your format to your strategy should be one of your first priorities, and a real no-brainer. However, in some cases the strategy might not have a huge bearing on this area, which then moves it into the "optional" territory. Tetley tea famously managed to engineer a huge boost in sales simply by making their tea bags round when everyone else's were square. It was completely functionless and un-strategic, but no matter; it proves how there is more untapped potential in this kind of thing than most brands realise.

- **Process innovation**. In theory you might be able to creatively execute your strategy in the way your product is made, rather than how it shows up on shelf / in the consumer's hands. The goal here is obviously to create a good story in an otherwise normal-seeming product. You've got to be careful, though, to ensure that the juice is worth the squeeze; do the punters really care? On the rare occasions they do this could be a good option.

- **Ritual innovation**. Some brands, particularly in alcohol, are able to build distinctive difference into the way consumers use the product via the addition of a ritual. Think of the lime in a Corona, or the repurposing of the otherwise unpopular

Jägermeister into a Jägerbomb. Coming up with the idea and actually getting people to play along are very different things, though, admittedly.

- **Brand proxies**. Finally, at the most ambitious level, is what Red Bull did, which was to essentially recognise they had no creative canvas within the product itself, and so built other things (events, sports, studios, etc.) within which to stretch their creative muscles. Basically this means doing something exciting separate to the core product and hoping that it elevates it by proxy. Clearly this can be fantastic, but let's face it, there's a reason why there aren't dozens of Red Bulls out there.

I'm not going to lie, it's pretty thin gruel. However, hopefully what I've demonstrated is that you might have to think a little laterally to come up with new territories for your canvas. Opportunity is not limited simply to what slaps you in the face. Unless you're a gym or airline, of course.

The correct use of a "why"

I've often been quite critical of the process of businesses "finding their why", largely because it's so often used as a substitute for developing a strategy. Although I think there are occasions when a "why" can double as a strategy, they are few and far between.

Where a "why" *can* be useful, however, is in strategic execution.

To understand why (ahem) this is, you need to first recognise that a "why" is at root a *leadership* tool. Its job is to inspire and motivate people – whether that's your team, your partners, or your customers. It's not the "what" or the "how" – that's the strategy. It's also not the explanation for why the strategy works, the rationale. That's also part of the strategy. It is instead the entirely separate question of *why it would be a good thing if we were to succeed with this strategy*.

Let me lay that out again like this:

What we're going to do, and why it will work —> Strategy
Why it would be a "good thing" if we were to do this
—> The "why"

(The way many businesses use the idea of "mission" is exactly the same; a mission is a why.)

As you can see, you don't need a why (or mission) for the strategy, and nor does it do a strategic job. It's an *additional* element which exists purely for propagandistic purposes. To "sell" the strategy to people, and to get them bought in.

You can see this clearly in the famous example of a why that Simon Sinek explained in his original TED talk. Here he described Apple's why as "we believe in challenging the status quo and thinking differently". OK, that stacks up, and clearly it was reflected in their "Think Different" strapline. However, you might also notice that this statement is entirely *strategically empty*. It doesn't tell you what part of the status quo they want to challenge, or *how* precisely they think differently. If Apple made computers out of cheese and forced all their employees to wear kilts, that would be "thinking differently and challenging the status quo". But it also wouldn't be very effective. What made them successful was the particular *way* they thought differently, and the why doesn't tell you that.

What the why does do, however, is to make those particularities (the strategy) sound noble and exciting. And this is very useful for execution.

By having a motivational why or crazy-sounding mission you will find it much easier to get your team aligned and on board. This is essential, as a common issue in strategy implementation is when teams think that the strategy is somehow "above them" and "belongs to the board", and isn't something that really concerns them at the coalface where they're doing the "real work" of the business. This is nonsense, clearly, because the strategy *manifests* at the coalface, meaning it's as much the concern of rank-and-file employees as it is anyone else.

A well-thought-out why serves to *connect* the strategy to such employees, and to make them feel that it's something they want to get involved with. It's also, frankly, going to be way more simple and one-dimensional than the strategy, making it easier to remember for those who aren't really strategically minded. Don't get me wrong: the strategy shouldn't be *complicated* – everyone should be able to get it easily – but being real, some people just aren't very interested in this kind of stuff and so will always be a tough audience. For them a why is a pretty good substitute. It won't tell them what to do and what's going on… but it will at least make them understand why the business is going through a process of change and will prevent all the annoying "what's the point of this" grumbles which can arise in any disruptive moment.

So how do you come up with one?

Well, it should go without saying that earning the business more money isn't a very effective why. Effective for you, maybe, but not effective for everyone else. No, instead there are three broad categories of why that you might consider:

1. Consumer benefit why
2. Category change why
3. Social good why

Consumer benefit why

A consumer benefit why is a pretty easy one to come up with, as it will fall directly out of a value-oriented strategy. Essentially the motivation is the good thing you're going to do for your consumers.

Now the catch here is that many great strategies won't have a particularly lofty or exciting benefit for consumers. The benefit might actually be something really quite humble but which nonetheless delivers real strategic advantage. Therefore don't assume that the benefit you're bringing to consumers will necessarily be powerful enough to act as a why for your team.

Category change why

When a consumer benefit why doesn't do the job, you should consider shifting to a category change one. In this instance you are essentially declaring your intention to "revolutionise" the category in some way. This may well feel bigger and more exciting than what you are doing for consumers, especially in a low-interest category where even the most outstanding value offering is going to be pretty trivial in the grand scheme of things.

Social good why

Finally we have the social good why, which naturally is what people typically imagine and tend to gravitate to first, since it's "noble" and therefore has strong motivational force behind it. And indeed, if you can claim that your strategy is going to have some wider social or ecological benefit – even as a by-product – then that's great. However, just be careful not to stray into the realms of parody here. Starbucks' mission (which is the same as a why in this instance) is to "inspire and nurture the human spirit", which, aside from being ridiculous on the face of it, isn't sufficiently connected to what the business actually *does* to be an effective motivational tool. At least not in my view.

You should easily be able to come up with a potential why in at least a couple of these areas if you have a good strategy, and then the job is simply picking the most exciting. Remember that unlike a strategy, a why doesn't necessarily have to be especially clever or unique. When you come right down to it, there are only really a few dozen broad variants of why that exist, because the things that move human beings are reasonably narrow and fixed. In all likelihood yours is going to be fairly similar to a lot of other businesses, and that's fine. What makes the difference is *how* you're going to go about achieving that lofty ambition – i.e. your strategy.

What I'd also recommend is quantifying it in some way, even if the numbers are basically bollocks. It just makes it feel more ambitious and tangible. So let's say in the case of Tesla – whose why / mission is "to accelerate the world's transition to sustainable energy" – you could push that further still by saying something like "to transition 100 million households to fully sustainable energy by 2040". It's not essential (certainly not for Tesla, who are fine on this front regardless), but in a lot of cases you can beef up a slightly feeble why this way.

Either way, much as it would be nice if a strategy were to sell itself, and act as its own motivational force, it ultimately needs to be combined with strong leadership – strong leadership from *you*. And a why is a tool to help you with that.

Keep moving to stand still: the trick to long-term execution

One big misconception people have about strategy is that you need to constantly re-do it as circumstances change. They think a strategy is something you have for two or three years, before getting a new one and moving on to that.

Although it's true that at a lower, more tactical, level there will be short- or medium-term priorities which come and go, at the highest, most truly strategic level things should *never* really change. Your strategy should be constant, lasting pretty much forever – unless there's some truly seismic market change.

This is especially true of the kind of value-based strategy we've been talking about in this book. This strategy defines *what your company is for* – and clearly, whatever this is, it shouldn't have a shelf life.

Your goal is to hold the same position indefinitely.

So how do we do this?

Well, this is where things get tricky. You see, it's easy to assume that in order to hold position and "stand still", you should do nothing. Just set your business up in its new strategic form, and let it coast that way forever. But sadly this isn't how it works. Because strategy is intensely contextual, you will need to constantly change the way you execute in order to hold the same position. As the world moves around you, what it takes to deliver on your value offering will shift, therefore demanding that you shift too if you don't want to accidentally transform into a very different business.

For an example of this, we can think about the post-Steve Jobs Apple. Jobs was unquestionably the strategic engine of that company, and for many years he guided them to create and dominate the world-changing position represented by products such as the original iMac, iPod, iPad, and iPhone. All of these products were accessible, democratic, and built entirely new consumer behaviours. When Jobs died, however, the business essentially became "locked in time". It continued to make "Jobs-esque" products but in a market context which had by now adjusted to them. As a result, although Apple remained essentially "the same", the company's market position drifted from (basically) "accessible" to "luxury". This hasn't been a commercial issue for the company at all – the success of the Jobs era essentially gave them default domination – but that's not the point. The point is that the company, by standing still and only really ever tinkering with its products, gradually adopted an entirely new strategy.

If you stand still but the market doesn't, your strategy will change without you knowing it.

Innocent, the UK juice and smoothie giant, is another example of this. When they first came on the scene, they represented the cutting edge of what passed for "healthy" and "pure" in UK supermarkets. This was in comparison to the market norm of products like Coke, against whom their difference was obvious. However, fast forward to present day, and the standards of what passes for "healthy and pure" have changed, and yet Innocent haven't. Rather than holding that part of the market they have been shunted to the centre ground. As with Apple, this isn't a problem for them, since they're now owned by Coke and are happy to reap profits as a mid-market player. But still, they aren't the brand they were before because, ironically, they *didn't* change.

The point here then is simply this:

You must keep moving in order to stand still.

You must constantly be re-executing your strategy in order to fulfil it in the latest market and cultural context.

An example of a brand who have done this well is Nike. Nike, unlike most of the other brands we've talked about here, have a very "brand-focused" strategy – meaning that they're fairly generic in other parts of their business, choosing instead to load all of their strategic leverage into their brand reputation. And to be fair, they've built arguably the most powerful brand image in the world, so you can't knock it. Anyway, the strategic territory they have tried to own for decades is one which we might call "the struggle". Whilst other athletic brands (when they launched) were obsessed with winning, glory, and all the fun parts of the athletic experience, Nike chose to be the brand for the darker moments. The pain and sweat of practice. The monotony of repetition. The fear of failure. This is what "Just Do It" is all about: overcoming these barriers and doing it anyway. Whether you win or lose is not the point. The enemy you're trying to overcome is yourself.

What's remarkable about this idea is how it's remained so fresh for basically half a century. Nobody looks at Nike and says, "OK, granddad, change the record." People still think they're cool. Why? Because they re-execute the strategy in a culturally relevant way *constantly*.

At the beginning, it was sufficient for them to focus simply on the ugly side of sport – early mornings, training in the rain, etc. Fast forward to now, however, and their focus recently has very much been on the social justice movements in which their athletes are engaged. Do you see how despite superficial differences this is all the same thing? How it's all still about "the struggle" and "overcoming"?

That's why Nike are arguably the greatest pure *brand* of all time. Relentless consistency, stretched over decades, grounded in frequent change.

What you need to get comfortable with then, is this blend of stasis and movement: stasis at the strategic level, movement at the executional level. A helpful way of visualising this can be done with something I call "multi-layer pacing", which is a fancy way of showing that the more strategic an element of the business is the *less* it changes, and the more tactical an element is the *more* it changes.

To see what I mean we must first divide a business into layers in descending from the strategic down to the tactical, something like this:

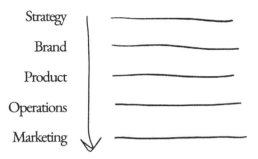

You can also think of this in terms of "big to small" or "macro to micro"; it's all the same thing. The point is the umbrella existential stuff at the top, and the day-to-day activities at the bottom. I've only done this example crudely to make the point, in reality there would probably be more layers than this, but whatever, you get the picture.

Now the idea with multi-layer pacing is that the pace of change for each of these layers is different: it speeds up as you go from top to bottom.

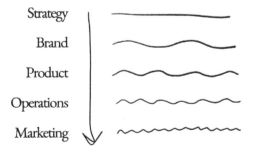

This serves as a basic illustration of how you want to think about executional change in your business over the years.

The macro strategy – "what the business offers in the market" – basically never changes. The brand below it will change a bit, but only very gradually. Think of the almost imperceptible evolution that's taken place with Nike and Red Bull; they keep things fresh but ultimately need to keep hold of their recognisable assets. Then, at the product level, if you're lucky changes won't have to happen very often either, but obviously you must be responsive to market trends (in a way that Innocent, say, weren't). You must always ensure your product delivers your value, and whether that requires frequent change or not doesn't really matter, just so long as you deliver. Operations then are naturally always in flux, not specifically for strategic reasons but more because that's just the way things are. And then naturally day-to-day marketing at a campaign level thrives off novelty and so changes a lot, even if the overall message remains static.

This then is the secret, not only to following a strategy but moreover doing it consistently over a long period of time. This consistency is what builds your brand reputation, and what gives you an unshakable stranglehold over your market position no matter what your competitors do.

When you first occupy a strategic position, that market space is still technically "up for grabs" even if you're the only company in it. Most consumers won't be aware of it or you, so in principle another brand could steal in there whilst everything's in a state of flux. However, the more time that passes with you holding steady, the less likely that is to happen – until you reach a point where you become inextricably associated with that position. At this moment a competitor could come along and even do it better than you, and it simply wouldn't matter. It's yours, thanks to your relentless consistency.

(This, incidentally, is another reason why "better" strategies don't work; because it's likely that the market position in question will already be held tightly by a big legacy brand, thus making any incursions into that territory futile.)

So never fall for the trap of novelty, of thinking you need to shake things up or move on to something fresh. Once you're strategically aligned, such things are pure vanity – done to satisfy you and not the customer.

What the customer wants is a clear, navigable market, with powerful brands holding position for decades.

So give it to them.

What now?

For now, this is all I can tell you.

Yes, there is much more to know, and many layers of subtlety and abstraction you can go into – but that's all refinement. What you've just read here are the need-to-knows, and with them you should in theory be able to develop a great strategy. Or at least a much better one than 99.99% of other people can.

As with any field of knowledge, true strength comes not from knowing a few facts or ideas, but rather from internalising them so you no longer have to think about them at all. So it's all just "there" intuitively. This is true of a particular strategy, and also of the field of strategy itself. That's why I write a free weekly newsletter, "The Hidden Path", which is all about gaining competitive advantage by seeing things others don't. By engaging with these ideas once a week, from different angles, you should be able to start developing that intuitive understanding.

To subscribe, just go here: www.basicarts.org/newsletter

I also publish daily thoughts and pointers on LinkedIn, so search for me there, Alex M H Smith, and hit "follow".

Finally, if you wanted to go even further and work together on developing a strategy – especially for a business that's already got a bit of traction – then why not get in touch? I'd love to hear from you.

Although you should now be able to do this on your own, it's by no means a guarantee that you actually will. There are many other factors that go into the success of a project than simple know-how. Just look at how much trouble people have losing weight, even though the information on how to do it is readily available. The knowledge is only part of the equation.

So if you want to explore this – or indeed ask me any other questions about what you've read here – then email me at contact@basicarts.org, or check out the website www.basicarts.org, where you'll find hundreds of articles that dig deeper into these topics.

Let us end, then, not by cursing the bullshit nature of most strategy but by showing gratitude for it. The more people misunderstand the field, and the more bad strategy there is out there, the more value can be accrued by the likes of you and me, who actually get it.

Because I promise you, even if you only skimmed this book...

...even if it went in one ear and out the other...

...even if you thought it was all nonsense...

...*even then* by this simple act of attention you now possess more strategic acumen and knowledge than anyone you're likely to encounter in everyday business.

And at the end of the day, that's gotta be pretty useful.

Alex

Made in the USA
Las Vegas, NV
03 October 2023

78503105R00085